I was sitting in this bar on [...]
midnight and I was in my usual com[...]
you know, nothing works right, the women, the jobs, the no
jobs, the weather, the dogs, the signs. Finally you just '
sit in a kind of stricken state and wait on the last death
like you're at a bus stop bench waiting on a bus. Well,
I was sitting there and here came this one with long dark
hair, a good body, sad brown eyes. I didn't light up for
her, I ignored her even though she had taken the stool next
to mine when there were a dozen other empty seats. In fact,
we were the only ones in the bar except for the bartender.
She ordered a dry wine. Then she asked me what I was drinking.

"Scotch and water."

"Give him a scotch and water."

Well, that was unusual.

"Thanks."

Then she opened her purse and took these little people
out and sat them on the bar. They were all around 3 inches
tall and they were alive and properly dressed. There were
4 of them, two men and two women.

"They make these now," she said. "They're very expensive.
They cost about 2,000 a piece when I got them. They go
for around 2400 now. I don't know the process and it's probably
against the law."

The little people were walking around the bar.
Suddenly one of the little guys slapped one of the little
women across the face.

"You bitch," he said,   "I've had it with you."

"No, Harry, you can't," she cried, "I love you. I'll
kill myself! I've got to have you!"

"And I don't care," said the little guy, and he took out
a tiny cigarette and lit it. "I've got a right to live."

"If you don't want her," said the other little guy,
"I'll take her. I love her."

"But I don't want you, Marty, I'm in love with George."

"But he's a bastard, Anna, a real bastard!"

"I know, but I love him anyhow."

CharlesBUKOWSKI
LAUGHINGwiththeGODS

Charles BUKOWSKI
LAUGHING with the GODS

INTERVIEW BY
Fernanda PIVANO

SUN DOG PRESS
NORTHVILLE, MICHIGAN

CHARLES BUKOWSKI: LAUGHING WITH THE GODS
Interview by Fernanda Pivano

Copyright © 2000 by Fernanda Pivano
Copyright © 2000 by Linda Lee Bukowski
Copyright © 1982 by SugarCo, Milano, Italy

Translated from the Italian by Fernanda Pivano and Simona Viciani

Cover Design by Grey Christian

Cover photograph of Bukowski and Pivano taken by Joe Wolberg in 1980, at Bukowski's home in San Pedro, California

Book design by Judy Berlinski

The publisher wishes to thank Daniel Waldron and Judy Berlinski for their professional help and guidance in the preparation of this book.

Warmest thanks to Linda Lee Bukowski for her enthusiasm for the project and providing clarification of the translation.

Also, grateful acknowledgement to: Simona Viciani for her excellent translation; Elfriede Pexa at the Living Literary Agency, Milano, Italy, who arranged the translation rights; and to Joe Wolberg for his photographs.

Thanks to Black Sparrow Press for permission to quote from *Reach for the Sun*.

This book was first published in a different version by SugarCo Edizioni S.r.l., Milano, Italia. Original title: Charles Bukowski: Quello Che Mi Importa E' Grattarmi Sotto Le Ascelle/Fernanda Pivano intervista Bukowski.

Library of Congress Cataloging-in-Publication Data

Bukowski, Charles.
  [Charles Bukowski. English]
  Charles Bukowski : laughing with the gods : interview / by Fernando Pivano; [translated from the Italian by Simona Viciani].
      p. cm.
  Includes bibliographical references and index.
  ISBN 0-941543-26-9
  1. Bukowski, Charles—Interviews. 2. Authors, American—20th century—Interviews. 3. Beat generation. I. Title: Charles Bukowski—laughing with the gods. III. Pivano, Fernanda. IV. Title.

PS3552.U4 Z46613 2000
811'.54—dc21
[B]
                                                    99-088647
Printed in the United States of America   First Edition

From a letter to John Martin
June 30, 1991

I'm glad I didn't quit. I'm glad I didn't toss it in. I still have the word. I work with it, play with it, it consumes me as it did then. I think the gods were playing with me. They still are. I'm going down to the last burning ember. The fire is hot. I have a small smile and the words leap onto the computer screen and I'm as young as I was then. There's no vanity attached, no wish for fame, just my guts pumping with the Word, one more, some more, the way I want it, the way it should be. I am
LAUGHING WITH THE GODS.

From the book: *Charles Bukowski: Reach for the Sun*
Black Sparrow Press, 1999

CONTENTS

INTRODUCTION

In 1980, the noted Italian writer and translator Fernanda Pivano came to the United States to interview Charles Bukowski. Her credentials as a literary Boswell were impressive. She had already interviewed, and written on Hemingway, Henry Miller, Jack Kerouac, Allen Ginsberg and others who have come to define modern American literature—introducing them to the Italian reader.

Her entree to Bukowski was provided by Joe Wolberg, a former philosophy professor who was manager of Ferlinghetti's City Lights bookstore.

Pivano visited Wolberg in San Francisco, where she was charmed by the novelty of a Mexican mariachi band, and enjoyed "sweet and delicious fruit" for breakfast at her hotel. Then the two flew to Los Angeles, and traveled in a rented car down to San Pedro where Bukowski's home was located. Ever the observing artist, she took note of the Hollywood scene, including its spiritual extension, Malibu, where F. Scott Fitzgerald had once lived.

What follows is, first, an account in her own words, of her journey to see Bukowski, who she notes "was called Hank by his friends, Charles by his editors, and Henry 'Hank'

Chinaski in his biographically-based works." Then she orients us with some facts about his life and publications. Then comes the lengthy, probing, and deeply revealing interview itself; and following this are insightful analyses that sharpen and enlarge our understanding of Bukowski and his writing. A look at the productions of stage and screen adaptations of Bukowski's work comes next, and finally a perceptive summing up.

In all, it is a remarkable document. Fernanda Pivano demonstrates how universal is Bukowski's appeal because she went home to Italy and published the book that follows in these pages. Its original was in Italian, of course. Translation into English has been made by Simona Viciani.

—Daniel Waldron/Editor

CharlesBUKOWSKI
LAUGHINGwiththeGODS

Interviews by Fernanda Pivano
San Pedro, California
August 24, 1980
April 14, 1984

1
GETTING THERE

Here's Malibu, a long windy stretch of sand sprinkled with some 400 luxurious homes for Hollywood's elite. This is where F. Scott Fitzgerald lived just before dying in a three-floor condo which, when a rock singer was living there in 1978, was set on fire by a pyromaniac.

All other traces of Fitzgerald's life there are erased forever; and already tiny condos have sprung up nearby for executives of the big movie studios who seek refuge from actors and directors. This is the other side of the coin of this half century of Hollywood's myths and legends.

From Malibu you pass eucalyptus blooming red along the roadside, gliders flying like sea gulls overhead, and a dedicated few windsurfing in the ocean. Eventually you come to the community of Pacific Palisades where Henry Miller died at the age of 88; and finally you arrive at Marina del Ray.

In Marina del Ray we were to meet Barbet Schroeder, the French film director, who lives in a jazz-era-style home on the beach with an entrance door protected by a metal screen that swung slowly in the wind. Schroeder is producing a 90-minute documentary about Charles Bukowski, and an hour-

and-forty-five-minute feature film called *Barfly*, with screenplay by Bukowski himself.

When we arrived, Barbet, handsome and charming, stood barefoot in the street, wrapped in a brown robe, as Californians sometimes wear, buying books from a seller who had spread his wares out on the ground, as in India. Barbet steered us around his huge American car and ushered us into his home. Immediately he showed us Bukowski—a Bukowski in color, speaking from the screen, big-nosed like a drunk, eyes narrowed like a hunted animal, a glass—almost symbolic—in his hand, his slow-moving body lounging in a wide armchair.

We spent hours watching Barbet's film footage, whiling away the afternoon to allow time for Bukowski to get home from the racetrack and Linda Lee from her vegetarian sandwich shop. Then Joe Wolberg and I got into the car we had rented in Los Angeles and headed for San Pedro. I was armed with my tape recorder and Joe with a set of exercise dumbbells he wanted to take to Bukowski. It had been years since Bukowski had said to his closest friends that when he reached 60 years of age he'd "start to get in shape;" and he turned 60 just a few days ago.

When we arrived in San Pedro we made a quick stop at a liquor store on the corner of the street where Bukowski has bought a home with a garden and a garage for his new BMW and his old Volkswagen— "all bought to get out of paying a few taxes," the writer says quite frankly.

We looked for the brand of German wine he is fond of now, having been advised that beer "is bad for him." Finally we arrived at his house, which is completely hidden by wildly growing flowering bushes. To get in we had to go through a driveway so narrow our car nearly scraped the walls on either side.

Linda Lee Beighle was working in the garden, her hands protected with big gloves. Under the name of "Sara" she is the main character in Bukowski's novel, *Women,* and for several years has been the mainstay of his life. The garden was full of fruit trees, rose bushes, and big yellow California flowers. A long metal lounge chair and other garden furniture completed the picture.

Beautiful, young, with that troubled albeit tender expression common to hippies, Linda Lee welcomed us. She took off her gloves and invited us inside, where we sat on wide American-style couches in the big California-suburban style sitting room. One of the couches facing the fireplace was a bit worn. Three cats prowled among the furniture: the white one was Linda's; the stray one had been starving when they picked it up from the street; and the most disreputable, the one they called "Butch Van Gogh," had been rescued from a cat-fight, having once belonged to "Sam, the Whorehouse Man."

On the fireplace mantel was a collection of sixty-one beer bottles, all different brands, one for each year of Bukowski's life plus one for good luck—or so said the friend who had given them to him.

Bukowski himself was not present. He was upstairs in the tiny room that must remind him of the rooms where he always lived in dramatic and perhaps productive poverty. There, with his typewriter, drunk every night (that's what he says), he writes his books. They are very popular. A couple of years ago, just on the income from the two books published by City Lights Books, he paid more in taxes than he had earned all his life.

Linda went to get him, and after a little while Bukowski appeared. He stopped at the door, and although his eyes were half-closed, they had the unmistakable look of someone who would rather be somewhere else. He was wearing sandals, a shirt with short sleeves, and Californian shorts which left his legs exposed. He is very proud of his legs and said "they are the only beautiful things I have."

He looked sideways at my recorder but smiled just the same. I had a note pad where I'd jotted down some questions in the car. He wanted to know what I was going to ask, and when he realized I didn't want to talk about literature and other writers he smiled again, and poured some wine into a fine crystal goblet.

The result of the interview is three hours of recording, seventy pages of manuscript, a big glass of raspberry juice after the distressing discovery that I don't drink alcohol, and two bottles of wine for him.

In the three hours of our interview, he didn't show a moment of weariness. His annoyance, if such there was, was well-hidden under his smiling mask. He never raised his voice and never displayed a sign of impatience—although toward the end he gave a nostalgic glance at the steps leading up to his room. It was so heartfelt, I took it as a signal to end the interview, so I made my farewell.

His goodbye was really kind. Bukowski kissed my hand like a Victorian gentleman; then he picked a rose from the bushes near the front door and gave it to me. As the car's engine started up he waved goodbye and said out loud, with a smile: "Write something nice!"

That's what I intend to do.

2
SOME FACTS

Biographies intrigue me a lot, but I won't try to write Bukowski's. Bukowski himself writes about his childhood and adolescence in *Ham on Rye*. Three volumes of stories, three novels, and a lot of poems give insight into his youth and mature age.

The dust jackets of his books have told us he was born on August 16, 1920, in Andernach, Germany. His family moved to the United States when he was two years old and brought him up in Los Angeles. Those are the bare facts. You have to read his stories and his numerous interviews to learn more about him.

You discover from his books, for instance, that his father was domineering and brutal. He severely beat his disobedient son during the boy's teenage years, thus condemning him to a state of unhappiness so deep, not even the financial success and the world-wide respect of later years could completely erase it. Instead of making him conform, the repression and strictness turned him into a rebel.

He started drinking at 13, seeking to find in alcohol, escape from the horrors of his family's treatment. His father didn't get the message. When his son came home drunk he would not let him into the house but forced him to sleep in the garage. Finally, the teenager turned against him by breaking down the door and punching the authority figure with his fist.

Was all of this true? Only Bukowski knows for sure. The image he has nurtured through the years has been that of the "tough man," even tougher than Hemingway, one who makes Humphrey Bogart look like a shy schoolboy. Is this truth or fiction?

We know his entrenched alcoholism is true. We know, also, that in his teens he was troubled by a very heavy form of acne that produced pimples so big, he says, they had to be opened by machine. Or is this a legend, too? Maybe he had smallpox. Maybe not. The deep marks that devastated his face are still visible today.

Eventually, Bukowski became a vagabond, supporting himself with bottom-rung jobs that Americans can find almost anywhere, lasting one day or one week. He worked in a slaughterhouse and as a whorehouse attendant. He was always drunk. He slept on park benches and in dingy hotels. He was jailed at one juncture for defying the authority of the army to conscript him for military service. When he was 34, he found himself close to death in a Los Angeles hospital, hemorrhaging because of drunkenness. Back on his feet, did he start a new life? No. He kept on drinking.

But now he was writing poems. He sent them to small magazines, sometimes the underground type and sometimes just the alternative kind. He lived in rooms that in reality were uninhabitable, in bad areas where he mingled with the underworld and lived out the notion of romantic but cursed poet which became the stuff of his poems and prose. By the time he got a job at the Los Angeles post office, he had hit bottom many times with the hardest, most dramatic, most negative experiences a man can have. He was 39 years of age.

The poems became well-known within his underground environment. His fame grew large because it was supported by the mystery that surrounded his life; Bukowski didn't know anyone and was not part of literary circles. For the first seven years of the 11 he worked in the post office, his only contacts with the literary world were the submission of poetry manuscripts to small and unknown magazines.

His fortunes began to rise in 1966 when John Martin, manager of an office supply and furniture company, bought five of his poems for broadsides. Martin gave Bukowski 30 dollars apiece—a godsend to the impoverished poet—and printed 30 copies of each edition. Two years later, in 1968, Martin published a further collection of Bukowski's poems under the title of *At Terror Street and Agony Way*. Seven hundred and fifty copies were sold in two months, who knows how? John Martin left his job to establish Black Sparrow Press and become a full-time editor and publisher, and Bukowski left his post office employment to become a professional writer. Martin had promised him a salary of one hundred dollars a month for the rest of his life. Bukowski was nearly 50.

Today Bukowski lives comfortably. John Martin remembers 1966 as "the year Mr. Rolls met Mr. Royce." But Bukowski's success was the result of a long period of writing apprenticeship before he ever met Martin. Small magazines and private printings were his outlets. He started in 1960 with *Flower, Fist, and Bestial Wail*. In 1962, *Poems and Drawings*, *Longshot Pomes for Broke Players*, and *Run With the Hunted* came out. They were republished in 1969 by Black Sparrow Press in Bukowski's first big collection of poems, *The Days Run Away Like Wild Horses Over the Hills*. In 1963, another small collection had been printed with the title *It Catches My Heart in Its Hands*, and in 1965 *Crucifix in a Deathhand*, from which in 1974 Black Sparrow Press chose ten poems for the first part of *Burning in*

Water, Drowning in Flame. This latter may be considered Bukowski's most important collection, 25 poems from it having been published in the *Penguin Modern Poets 13.*

In 1965 the collection of poems, *Cold Dogs in the Courtyard* and a collection of stories, *Confessions of a Man Insane Enough to Live with Beasts*, had been published. *Cold Dogs . . .* was republished in *The Days Run Away Like Wild Horses Over the Hills* and *Confessions. . .* in 1973's collection, *South of No North.* That same collection included "All the Assholes in the World and Mine," which first came out in 1966.

Not reprinted until now are "The Genius of the Crowd," a poem published in a 1966 chapbook, and a small collection published in 1968, *Poems Written Before Jumping Out of an 8th Storey Window.* The two small collections that came out in 1967, *2 by Bukowski* and *The Curtains Are Waving*, were reprinted in *Burning in Water, Drowning in Flame*, together with *At Terror Street and Agony Way*—the 750 copies of which, as we have seen, marked the start of Bukowski's fortune.

Throughout those years, underground magazines multiplied steadily in the United States, and it was in them, through his articles and stories, that Bukowski built a loyal and growing audience. His stories appeared in such publications as *Nola Express, Evergreen Review, Knight, Pix, Berkeley Barb, Adam, The Adam Reader* and others, including one that was to play a significant part in his career. In 1968, John Bryan, who had built circulation of the underground *Los Angeles Free Press* from 16,000 to 48,000 copies, left that paper and started *Open City.* He asked Bukowski to become a columnist for it. Bukowski hesitated, then sent a single article instead. It was a review of *Papa Hemingway*, a volume of memories by A. E. Hotchner. Soon after that review, Bukowski began writing a regular column for *Open City.* He called it "Notes of a Dirty Old Man," which further spread his fame as an underground character.

22

The hearsay and facts about Bukowski's life are as crazy and strange as the stories he writes. In a certain way Bukowski is a legend in his own time: a recluse, a lover, tender, vicious, horrible, a saint . . . The jury is still out. It seems there is no middle ground. People love him or hate him. Only one thing is sure: you can't read him and remain the same.

Pivano interviews Bukowski at his home in San Pedro, California, 1980.

Photo: Linda Lee Bukowski

3

INTERVIEW (1980)

Interview with Charles Bukowski
San Pedro, California
Sunday, August 24, 1980
Fernanda Pivano

CHARLES BUKOWSKI: What was the first question?

FERNANDA PIVANO: I was thinking of asking you what you think of the image that the media has made of you?

BUKOWSKI: Well, you see, I'm not quite sure what image the media has made of me because—especially in Europe, I don't read the reviews because they're in a different language. So, I have no idea what's happening over there. All I know is the books are starting to sell, but what they're saying about me, I don't know. I only speak English; I only read English. So, you know what's happening more than I do. How's that?

PIVANO: And how about the image they make of you in America?

BUKOWSKI: Well, ah, it's a little over-exaggerated—that I'm a tough guy, and I jump in and out of bed with all the ladies, and all that. They're a little behind times on me. I used to do that to an extent, but generally they've over-exaggerated. They've exaggerated what I am, what I did, what I do. It's a little hyped-up. *Hyped-up*, that's not an Italian phrase. (laughter) To have the best image of me, the true image, they must simply read what I've written and not make up their minds outside of the books.

PIVANO: But is what you have written so autobiographical that it might give an image of your life?

BUKOWSKI: Yes, it's pretty close to what's happened. Yeah, it's ninety-five percent truth and five percent fiction. It's just polished up a bit, around the edges. But you see, a lot of women hate me, because they've heard that I do all these bad things to the female, you see? But many of them have never read my books, it's just word-of-mouth, that I'm this terrible person who mutilates women, beats them, pisses on them, and all that. But very few of them have read my works. But if they did, they'd realize that often I was the one who got pissed on or mutilated by the female. So I, and also . . .

PIVANO: When you say female, you mean feminist, or just female?

BUKOWSKI: Just female. I don't go to bed with feminists. And often in my works, *I* look to be the fool more often than the woman. But even those females who read my works, can't seem to pick up on this kind of thing. They only see when the woman looks bad. That's all their eyes can see, their minds can pick up. But when *I* look bad, it's overlooked. So, I think there's an unfair opinion of me—but I don't care, because it helps sell the books, you know. It's an exaggerated idea of what I am. It makes me more sensational than I am, more of a bastard than I am. Which all helps to sell books, because people who tend to hate you are good readers too. They're very curious when they hate. So, this false image all helps sales.

PIVANO: Helps sales?

BUKOWSKI: Yes. I see you've got your little machine going.

PIVANO: That's not what I think that you writers, you poets, you public figures, or whatever you want to call yourselves, are so accustomed to.

BUKOWSKI: Accustomed to what?

PIVANO: To the machines, to the recorder. You really don't care any more for that.

BUKOWSKI: Well, yeah, I've been interviewed, I guess, over a hundred times.

PIVANO: Yes, so that you don't care any more.

BUKOWSKI: I hardly care to answer the questions correctly. But I'll try. (laughter)

PIVANO: Because you don't care for the questions? Is that what you mean?

BUKOWSKI: No, no, it isn't that. It's just, you keep hearing similar questions, it's . . .

PIVANO: All the same.

BUKOWSKI: Yes, they're basically, well, they have to be the same. So, please go ahead.

PIVANO: And so, this is more or less the same question—what do you think of the macho figure that you make of yourself in your books? Not what the media are doing. Are you really as macho as you want to show in your books?

BUKOWSKI: Well, I don't show anything except what's occurred. So if you want to call it macho, from what you read, then I'm macho, because everything that I've written, I'd say, is ninety-five percent true. So, if the writing appears macho, then I'm macho. I plead guilty.

PIVANO: And what is macho for you?

BUKOWSKI: What is it for you? I mean, you're the one who is . . .

PIVANO: No, I want to know what it is for you, to know if my question has any meaning.

BUKOWSKI: Well, if you think I'm macho from what you've read of me and my books, that's macho—what I've written. I'm macho. In other words, we have a circle going.

PIVANO: Yes. Have you ever had any struggle with the feminists? I know that you don't go to bed with them. And, I'm not a feminist, please. So let's start at the beginning again.

BUKOWSKI: Well, *we're* not going to bed.

PIVANO: But have you ever had any discussion with the feminists?

BUKOWSKI: Well, weren't we picketed in Germany somewhere? I'm always drunk, you see. Linda said it was *one* girl. I was very excited. I came out drunk, thinking there were five or six there, with "Bukowski's a Macho Pig" posters. (laughter)

LINDA LEE BEIGHLE: I didn't want to burst your bubble.

BUKOWSKI: It was only one?

L. LEE: But she was enough for a whole team, because she was just screaming and yelling: "You macho pig, you son-of-a-bitch macho male chauvinist pig."

BUKOWSKI: I don't know what makes them angry. I don't quite understand it. It just makes me smile. I don't know, really.

L. LEE: They think you're a womanizer and all that.

BUKOWSKI: I really don't get it. I've written quite a number of love stories that are just total love stories, simply that. I guess they don't read those. And then, now and then, I'll be attacked. This girl in Germany was screaming at me? Calling me all sorts of things in the hotel where I sang?

L. LEE: Yes.

BUKOWSKI: I just see the mouth going and the hatred. I don't know what they're . . . They show up now and then, and they really seem to hate me.

PIVANO: Well, the feminists have some reason to hate you.

BUKOWSKI: Really?

PIVANO: The feminist, not the woman.

BUKOWSKI: Oh, oh. Well, why do the feminists hate me? I'm curious.

PIVANO: You know much better than I.

BUKOWSKI: What have I done? No, I have no idea.

PIVANO: You have written the books that you have written.

BUKOWSKI: Yeah? —and that's it?

PIVANO: Yes. (laughter) I think it is plenty. Don't you think it is plenty? Poor feminists.

BUKOWSKI: I'm just writing about men and women. I'm writing about both.

PIVANO: Yes, but the image that you give of women is not the image that the feminists would like to be spread around as women, you know.

BUKOWSKI: These are the women I've met and what we've done together.

PIVANO: Yes.

BUKOWSKI: We've had some pretty interesting times.

PIVANO: This is clear. This is absolutely clear. Yes, no doubt.

BUKOWSKI: I'm really confused about what they object to. I'm really sincere, I don't know what bothers them. I have no idea what bothers them. I really don't, Joe. I don't know what the hell bothers them.

JOE WOLBERG: I think you're right that most of them just simply haven't read the work because what they're reacting to—I know what they're reacting to: they're reacting to an *audience* you have—of people who misinterpret your work, who are, in some way, gross slugs who identify with some kind of weird image they have of you. And so, what these feminists are really protesting or reacting to is a certain kind of person or audience that identifies with you. But you see, anarchists have identified with him, fascists have identified with him.

PIVANO: FASCISTS?

BUKOWSKI: I get letters . . .

PIVANO: How could fascists identify with you?

BUKOWSKI: I guess they think, from certain parts of my writing, that I'm one of them.

PIVANO: Which part of your writing? I didn't find any fascist part in your writing.

BUKOWSKI: I guess there are parts where I talk about Adolf Hitler, at times—in my early youth, I pretended to be a Nazi. They probably identify with that.

PIVANO: Here in America?

BUKOWSKI: Yeah. When I was going to college.

PIVANO: You were meaning it?

BUKOWSKI: No, I was pretending to be a Nazi.

PIVANO: And why did you pretend to do such a horrible thing?

BUKOWSKI: There was—it wasn't so horrible, I was simply bored because everybody else was pro-war, everybody else was going in one direction.

PIVANO: Which was a way of being anti-American.

BUKOWSKI: It was just a way of not being one of them. I guess there's a thing in a lot of writers, when they see the whole crowd going this way, they automatically want to go the other way. That's why they're writers. They're strange creatures. I guess, maybe, Celine got burned this way a bit and Knut Hamsun, and Ezra Pound, and a lot of writers. I don't think they really believed in fascism or Nazism, but simply because everybody was going one way they couldn't stand it. They had to go a little bit the other way. I don't expect you to understand that.

PIVANO: You know that I jump when I hear that.

WOLBERG: But he was put in jail, too, for the same thing.

PIVANO: For which thing?

32

BUKOWSKI: I have no idea what he's talking about.

WOLBERG: Well, you . . . weren't you put in . . . didn't they arrest you because you didn't want to go?

BUKOWSKI: No, this was simply because I didn't give a damn. I was drinking all the time; I didn't read the instruction from my draft board. It never said come and be inducted, it said something like—you must inform *us* when you change your address—not the post office. I informed the post office. I thought, well, if they want me, they can find me. So I was a draft dodger.

PIVANO: And so you were drafted and you didn't go?

BUKOWSKI: They threw me in jail and then they put me in front of . . . you know, you have to pass the psychiatrist. So I was safe. I couldn't get passed by him. He asked me three questions. He said, "Do you believe in the war?" I said, "No." He said, "You're willing to go to the war?" and I said, "Yes." You know a guy's crazy. (laughter)

PIVANO: If he doesn't believe it, but he'll go?

BUKOWSKI: But I meant these; I was not joking. And then he asked his third question. He said, "By the way, I know you're a very intelligent man. We're having a party at my house next Wednesday night. Writers, artists, painters. I want to invite you to my party. Will you come?" I said, "No." He said, "All right. You can go." (laughter) All I had to do was say yes—wait . . . no, yes, yes.

PIVANO: No. No, yes, no.

BUKOWSKI: Do you believe in the war? No. Willing to go? Yes. Oh. No. Yes. No.

PIVANO: And why did you want to go to the war?

BUKOWSKI: Well, I figured it would be interesting. You know, men would be killed for no reason at all, and maybe I would be killed, maybe I would kill somebody. I had no beliefs at all, it would be kind of like a circle, you see. I wouldn't mind the killing, being killed wouldn't bother me. The main reason I didn't want to go was because I don't like to be in a large room or confined with many men. It's . . . ah . . . I lose my individuality. I just didn't want to march with the fellows up and down; I didn't want to get drunk with them on leave; I didn't want to go out with them and look for a piece of ass. But to kill or be killed wouldn't bother me.

PIVANO: I understand that to be killed doesn't bother you, but to kill is . . .

BUKOWSKI: To kill? Wouldn't bother me either, because I'm forced into this situation and they tell me I'm doing a good thing. Okay. I'll do the good thing.

PIVANO: But you finished saying that not to do and think what the other people were thinking and doing made you pretend that you were a Nazi. So, why did you accept the fact that if they tell you to kill it was okay to kill?

BUKOWSKI: But I'm killing for a different reason than the guy next to me is killing. He's killing because he believes in killing. I'm killing because it doesn't matter. My reason is different. It serves the same purpose.

PIVANO: Yes. I would like to ask you something about the documentary I saw, in part, this morning. They showed me only a very small part. You were speaking of style. The comparison between style and truth.

BUKOWSKI: Oh, I was? You know, I drink when these things are going on, so I don't know or remember what I said.

Wolberg: You said that style was more important than truth.

PIVANO: But I did not quite realize what you meant by style. Was it as Hemingway referred to style—as a way of life, or the style in which we . . .

BUKOWSKI: Well, let's leave Hemingway out of it. Style—I probably meant writing style, living style, whatever you're doing.

PIVANO: Probably living style, because you were mentioning it connected with truth.

BUKOWSKI: Well, truth has a way of changing every day, every second. You hold on to your style, truth changes around you. While you have style, you have your own method going, while other things are wavering. Follow?

PIVANO: Yes.

BUKOWSKI: That's about it. It's quite simple.

PIVANO: But the living style? Does it change also?

BUKOWSKI: Mine doesn't change too much. I just drink different stuff.

PIVANO: But one must think of living style. Do you identify your living style with drinking?

BUKOWSKI: I get up at the same time. Oh, yes, that's part of it.

PIVANO: Then you drink as a choice?

BUKOWSKI: The main part.

PIVANO: As a choice of a way of living?

BUKOWSKI: Well, do I shit as a choice?

PIVANO: Well, you cannot help shitting, but you can help the . . .

BUKOWSKI: I can't help drinking, either. I'd die if I stopped either one, you see. One way or another I would die. I drink when I write. Or, do I write when I drink? You see?

PIVANO: Yes.

BUKOWSKI: And writing is ninety percent of me. The other ten percent is waiting around to write. Got it?

PIVANO: Yes. You also said in the documentary that nature is very cruel, or something like that—not exactly in those words. You said it much louder. Can you tell me something about your idea on nature?

BUKOWSKI: I have no ideas on nature. I mean, nature doesn't thrill me, you see.

PIVANO: It doesn't?

BUKOWSKI: No. Like the flowers, and the birds, and the bees, and the magic of things growing. It's all right, see. Or ... ah ... when the panther kills something, it doesn't thrill me. All this mechanism of nature has been here a long time. I mean, it doesn't excite me too much. It's a thing like a next-door neighbor, I live with it.

PIVANO: But, if nature doesn't thrill you, how come you choose to live in such a beautiful place? With all the trees and flowers?

BUKOWSKI: That's for tax purposes, my dear. (laughter) If I didn't buy this house the government would take my money away, and I'd still be living in a small room. I would never live in a place like this of my own choice. I have lived through all my life in tiny rooms. A house gives you a tax write-off.

PIVANO: But a house should have a garden to lower taxes?

BUKOWSKI: I hate lawns, because I used to have to mow the lawn when I was a boy—both ways.

PIVANO: You worked outside? You?

BUKOWSKI: For a long time there was nothing out there but dirt.

PIVANO: Yes?

BUKOWSKI: I'm not a gardener.

PIVANO: But now you like lawns? . . . or not?

BUKOWSKI: Oh, I hate lawns. Everybody has a lawn with grass.

PIVANO: Oh, you hate that because everybody has . . .

BUKOWSKI: I hate lawns because everybody does it. People have lawns in front of their houses because they don't have time to do anything else. They have their jobs, so they have to cover the ground with something that doesn't bother them too much. So a lawn is an American way. I don't know about Europe. But here, everybody has a lawn. And when you tend to do the same things everybody else does, you become everybody else.

PIVANO: Do you think this attitude you have is connected to an anarchist's attitude or just an individualistic attitude.

BUKOWSKI: It was caused when I was a child. My father made me mow a goddamned lawn. And trim it. I had to mow every blade of grass, both ways. So they were all even. Perfectly even. If one blade of grass was sticking up, I would get a beating. It has nothing to do with anarchy. I just don't want to mow a lawn. It's a bad memory. But the anarchists identify with me too. Why, I don't know, either.

PIVANO: The question was in reference to the time that you said you don't want to do things that everybody does. That you don't like doing things that everybody does.

BUKOWSKI: Mostly so, but I shit, yes, and I eat twice a day, I take baths, I do many things other people do. But there are many things people do that I don't do. I didn't have a television set until I was fifty years old. Maybe I'm weakening, you see.

PIVANO: I must confess to you that I don't have a television set and I'm sixty-three.

BUKOWSKI: Oh-oh, she's topped me. Well, have you ever had one?

PIVANO: No, because my mother had one. But I never had one.

BUKOWSKI: Oh.

PIVANO: So now we make friends, yes?

BUKOWSKI: Oh, I thought we were!

PIVANO: Yes, I'm joking. The impression someone might have from your books is that, in a way, you don't love life. You live, but without loving living. Is that a bad impression? A wrong impression?

BUKOWSKI: No, it's pretty accurate. I find life fairly uninteresting, and I especially did when I was working the eight-hour day and the twelve-hour day. Most men work the eight-hour day at least five days a week. And they don't love life either. There's no reason for a man who works eight hours a day to love life. You sleep eight, you work eight. I discussed this with a friend of mine once, and we figured out a man working eight hours a day with all the extra things he has to do—like get a drivers' license, new tires for his car, fight with his girlfriend, shop for groceries—only has two hours or an hour and a half at leisure to himself. He can only live, truly, one and one-half hours a day and you give all the other hours away. This is what I had to do most of my life. And I didn't love this. I think any man who loves this is a big idiot. There's no way I could love that kind of life.

PIVANO: And, how about now?

BUKOWSKI: It's getting better.

PIVANO: So now you start loving life?

BUKOWSKI: No. I'm very wary of loving life, because it may fool me if I start loving it. So, I'm very cautious about such matters. I'm still watching everything.

PIVANO: But now you don't have to work eight hours a day.

BUKOWSKI: Now I work every hour of the day.

PIVANO: But you are not compelled to. You work because you love the work that you do. You love writing. Don't tell me that you don't love writing.

BUKOWSKI: I like drinking, and I write when I drink, sometimes. No, writing isn't work at all, you're right. And when people tell me how painful it is to write, I don't understand it, because it's just like rolling down the mountain, you know. It's freeing. It's enjoyable, it's a gift, and you get paid for what you want to do.

PIVANO: I don't think you write because you are getting paid for writing.

BUKOWSKI: No, I write because it comes out—and then to get paid for it afterwards? I told somebody, at some time, that writing is like going to bed with a beautiful woman, making love to her, and when you get up, somebody hands you some money. It's just too much. Of course you take the money, because you need it. That's all. Anything else?

PIVANO: About the love for life?

BUKOWSKI: I thought I expressed that. Most men are caught in this workaday world. And men do get to love their jobs, because that's all there is. I mean, they take pleasure in doing these monotonous jobs. They actually take pride in doing this stuff. Well, they can love it. I never did love those jobs. I had about fifty, a hundred, a hundred and fifty jobs. I disliked them all—I realized I was being raped.

PIVANO: But it never happened that you woke up one morning and—thank you very much—looked out the window to see the sky without the clouds and were happy?

BUKOWSKI: And to see a little bird flying by? No.

PIVANO: It might be the bird would be too much. (laughter)

BUKOWSKI: You've already given me too much without the bird. No, looking at the clouds going by and the blue sky, no. Actually, if I liked something, it would be a dark thundershower with black clouds, yeah.

PIVANO: Dark? You like that?

BUKOWSKI: A thunderstorm with the rain coming down, and lightening. Closer to the Devil, you see.

PIVANO: You feel yourself closer to the Devil?

BUKOWSKI: Actually, I'm more in sympathy with the Devil than I am with the nice guys. He seems a more interesting fellow to me down there burning in these flames. He lost the battle with God and he got tossed down there in these flames. Maybe I can help him out of there and we'll take over, and change things a little.

PIVANO: When did you start feeling close to the Devil?

BUKOWSKI: This is mostly a joke. I hardly think of it that way. But when you brought up the light clouds and the blue sky, I started thinking of the Devil just to counteract the light clouds and the blue sky. You see, I react a great deal. Touch me here, and this arm will jump out. I react. It could be largely defensive. Whatever it is, it is. There is a poem I wrote. It's called, "I Met a Genius." And it was about a sadomasochist little boy on the train, we're going to the racetrack. And we're both looking at the water—you know, the waves breaking, and he turns to me and says, "It's ugly, isn't it?" And I say, "That's the first time I realized that." I just thought it was nothing up until then, just water doing nothing.

WOLBERG: This is John Martin's—it may be one of John Martin's favorite poems.

PIVANO: And when did this take place?

BUKOWSKI: This happened . . . When did it happen? A long time ago. Years. I don't know. Twenty-five or thirty years ago?

PIVANO: And so this is when you started acknowledging the fact that you were not loving nature?

BUKOWSKI: I never acknowledge facts, or I don't go about thinking "I don't love nature," or "I do love nature." I don't go around accumulating facts of myself. Most of the time I don't think at all. I'm kind of . . .

PIVANO: Living.

BUKOWSKI: No, not living, just, well, we have a term here in America we call "spaced." You just go—oh, okay, all right. You really don't get involved. There's too much happening all the time. Even when you're sitting still, things are happening. You don't have to look for anything, you don't have to appreciate anything, things are just occurring all the time. Just lifting a glass of wine and drinking it is enough. That's why I hate to travel to Europe—see the towers and structures. I don't need that. Everything's occurring already. I don't have to go somewhere and look at things. I don't have to look at the water and say: "Oh, look at the motion." I don't have to say, "Look at the cat. Look at the cat shit." Now and then I do, but most of the time there's nothing to say, nothing to do until I sit down to the typewriter and then it comes out. I'm not a thinking man.

PIVANO: How come you have three cats?

BUKOWSKI: Well, one of the cats belongs to Linda, so when we got together, there's one cat automatically, it comes with the lady, right? Okay. The other one belonged to Sam, the

Whorehouse Man. He went crazy and so we brought Butch here with us. He's the one with one ear. Then the third cat just walked through. He was starving to death. You can disregard many things, but when a cat loses that voice and you can see his bones sticking through his fur, you at least feed it, right? I mean, we're not that indifferent. So, you feed a cat like that once, it's going to stay. I have no excuse for having three cats. (laughter)

PIVANO: I was making the connection between the fact that you don't love nature and the little birds, but you love cats.

L. LEE: And you become very upset when you see one of the cats bring a bird in, in its mouth.

BUKOWSKI: That's why I don't love nature, see?

L. LEE: It kills each other.

PIVANO: Yes, because nature is cruel.

BUKOWSKI: Sometimes, yeah.

PIVANO: But I am sure you never heard of an Italian poet of a long, long time ago, two centuries ago, called Leopardi.

BUKOWSKI: No.

PIVANO: Because he put up a philosophy about the cruelty of nature. He might be of some interest to you, maybe. It might be of some interest to you, maybe.

BUKOWSKI: Oh, I'm not that bothered by the cruelty of nature. It doesn't bother me that much. It's just when people say, "Oh, isn't nature beautiful?" I say, "Yes, if you think so." I mean, I don't walk around thinking nature is cruel. I don't write poems about it. I think you're making too much of it. I don't think about nature. I think *well, I'm going to the harness' races next Tuesday afternoon.* I don't have grand thoughts, I don't have large thoughts of a philosophical nature. I'm a very simple man and when I write poems, they're about simple things. And I guess this is why a lot of people who can't read most poets, read my stuff. They understand what I'm talking about.

PIVANO: What do you like better, to write poems or to write fiction?

BUKOWSKI: Well, it depends upon my mood. The poem is always the easiest thing to write, because you can write it when you're totally drunk or when you're totally happy or totally unhappy. You can always write a poem. So a poem is very handy; it's an emotional expression that just pops up. Fiction or short story—I have to feel very good to write that. So it's up to me, it depends upon the mood. If I'm feeling good, I can write fiction; if I'm feeling good, I can write a poem. But if I'm feeling bad, see, the only difference is, if I'm not feeling very good, I can write a lot of poems. I've written thousands of poems through most of my life. So, you see how I felt.

PIVANO: What are the things that make you happy and the things that make you unhappy? Success in love, love-making, I mean?

BUKOWSKI: Oh, no, no, that's one of the least things that I worry about.

PIVANO: What are they? So, what are the things that make you happy and unhappy.

BUKOWSKI: Well, I guess going to the racetrack, and picking seven winners out of nine.

PIVANO: Don't make fun of me.

BUKOWSKI: I'm serious. I tell Linda—it's like magic. You see all these horses . . .

L. LEE: He's not, it's true.

BUKOWSKI: . . . and I say: Number Six. And Six comes in. They give me money. It's not exactly the money, but the money's approved. And many days are like that. You just go like that, and here comes the horse. It's like a magic trip. It's so . . .

WOLBERG: Hank has a system too. He has *systems.*

BUKOWSKI: Thousands.

WOLBERG: And the system has to do with betting against the masses of people. The system is very much like that other line of thought . . . that's against the crowd.

BUKOWSKI: Yeah, a reversal. I bet the slowest horse I can find—the worst looking horse at the shortest price I can get. In other words, I reverse everything. And I do much better than most people.

PIVANO: And what would make you unhappy?

BUKOWSKI: Ah . . . giving interviews.

PIVANO: Thank you.

BUKOWSKI: Having hangovers, when my feet hurt. My feet hurt an awful lot. I guess the thing that makes me most unhappy is being in a crowd of people—a large crowd of people, and listening to their conversations. It really makes me unhappy—not only unhappy, but it almost drives me insane. Because here's all of humanity and I'm stuck in the center of them and this is all they can say. To me, this makes me very unhappy.

PIVANO: Because the conversation is banal?

BUKOWSKI: It's worse than banal. It's inane. It's . . . dogs talk better, and they can't even talk. Yes, banal. I don't like crowds, crowded places. I used to pull down all the shades, not answer the doorbell, knocks, or any of it for a week at a time. Just lay in bed alone. To see nobody, to do nothing. It's very fulfilling to me.

WOLBERG: You think that's just an idiosyncrasy of your own personality, or is that a requirement for writers? For a good writer?

BUKOWSKI: I think it's just my personality.

WOLBERG: So you don't fault other writers—someone like Ginsberg, who really likes to be in crowds, it would seem—for being that way.

BUKOWSKI: Well, I guess he picks up energy from the crowd. He picks up what I lose in the crowd. He picks up, so I'd leave him his crowds.

PIVANO: And do you think that this is the reason why you chose to come and live in such a secluded place?

BUKOWSKI: Oh, yes, of course. San Pedro is a wonderful place. I would not live in San Francisco, New York City, since I have a choice. Even when I lived in Los Angeles, it was a particular district—where the poor people were.

PIVANO: You lived in Hollywood, did you?

BUKOWSKI: East Hollywood, a great deal of the time. Usually in a court with its own front door.

WOLBERG: Yeah, the image you have of Hollywood is probably not like the place he lived in. All the doors are off the hinges; people are shooting each other and screaming.

BUKOWSKI: Cockroaches.

WOLBERG: Whores, junkies . . .

PIVANO: But then you lived there because you had no choice.

BUKOWSKI: Well, I might have lived in a better neighborhood, if I'd looked around and really tried. Like—certain people would

48

never live where I've lived, just because they think this type of place is horrible. I rather liked it, because I didn't have to deal with the standard type of person. "Good morning, this is a nice day, today." I didn't have to bother with that, you see. I'm not in love with humanity, you see?

PIVANO: Yes, that is what is clear from your books. But I wonder . . . the roots. Where are the roots of it? Where did it start? Why are you not in love with humanity?

BUKOWSKI: Let's see . . . I never analyze, I just react. If I don't like something, I stay away from it. But I never try to figure it out: "Why don't I like this?" I go with my prejudices. I never try to improve myself, or try to learn anything, I just remain exactly the way I am. I'm not a learner; I'm an avoider.

PIVANO: You are not a learner, you're an avoider.

BUKOWSKI: Yes. I don't want to learn. I feel perfectly normal in my own mad way.

PIVANO: But what do you avoid?

BUKOWSKI: Becoming others.

PIVANO: And you think if you learn about yourself, you become an "other"?

BUKOWSKI: If I went to a psychiatrist and found out where all my wires crossed, and got all my wires straightened out, why, I think I'd start patting children on the head, and smiling at apple trees, then go upstairs to type. I'd write crap that nobody would ever read, because it would be what everybody else was saying or doing or pretending to say and do. When I go up to write, it is what I am now. Untampered with.

PIVANO: So, let's try this problem from another side.

BUKOWSKI: Problem?

PIVANO: Yes, for me. Not so for you. When did you start finding out that you were not loving humanity?

BUKOWSKI: My grandmother said that when I was very small, she leaned over the cradle to kiss me and I punched her in the nose. (laughter) That was probably the first human face that I saw. So, then, you look at your parents and wonder: what are these big, tall, dumb things that have power over you?

PIVANO: Oh, because they have power. You don't like that they have power.

BUKOWSKI: No, I want the power, don't you? So, then you go to grammar school, and that's a horror trip. Because, here are all these people the same size as you, and they're doing all these silly things: bouncing balls around and screaming things. They're idiots. I used to look at them and say, "What's wrong with them?" And they'd look at me and say, "Hey, there's something wrong with you." The crowd was always here, and I was always there, from the very beginning. And there's just an impasse. It's the same now when I give a poetry reading. They come to see me, but I am myself and they are something else, and we're still fighting each other, you see? And they know that, and there's a reaction coming out.

PIVANO: Are you going to tell lovemaking stories, even in your childhood? When did you start making the lovemaking scene?

BUKOWSKI: Well, when I was—I think I had my first woman when I was twenty-three years old.

PIVANO: Twenty-three?

BUKOWSKI: Yes.

PIVANO: So that's why you made up for all the time you lost before.

BUKOWSKI: That's true, I guess, That's when I wrote *Women* you know, meeting all these women. I guess it was about a five year period. Then I went through that and I said, "I don't need all this. It's not what it's supposed to be."

PIVANO: And what were you doing before going with women? Until twenty-three? You were going with boys?

BUKOWSKI: Oh, no, no, dear.

PIVANO: You never had this experience?

BUKOWSKI: I would just drink. Drink.

PIVANO: Even so young, even as a boy?

BUKOWSKI: Beer, wine, anything I could get hold of. It was nice, it made life interesting.

PIVANO: And when did you come—this is biographical information that I should have, that I don't have—when did you come in to San Pedro, to live in San Pedro?

BUKOWSKI: Two years ago? I've lost track.

PIVANO: So you came when you started having your success—your writing, your money, let's say.

BUKOWSKI: Tax write-off, you know. That's why I had to buy the car that's in the garage.

PIVANO: Why did you have to buy the car? Because you were living here?

BUKOWSKI: No, it's another tax write-off.

PIVANO: So if you buy a car, you pay less taxes?

BUKOWSKI: Yes.

PIVANO: Ah, I didn't know that.

WOLBERG: Half the price of the car would go to taxes anyway, so you might as well buy the car.

PIVANO: Yes, I understand.

WOLBERG: Not only that, but he likes this car, too, so don't let him get away with that. (laughter)

PIVANO: What car is it?

BUKOWSKI: BMW . . .

PIVANO: BMW? And you drive it? You learned how to drive it?

BUKOWSKI: Oh, I've had cars, but they've all been very old cars.

PIVANO: But are you accustomed to drive?

BUKOWSKI: Oh, yes, I've driven other cars.

WOLBERG: He just bought that. When I first knew him, he had just bought a Volkswagen and he was so happy to have that Volkswagen.

BUKOWSKI: That was one of the best cars.

WOLBERG: And he was so careful with it.

PIVANO: Yes, it's very nice, yes. And you can put lots of baggage in it. It's incredible how much luggage you can put in a Volkswagen. It's the most intelligent car you can have, yes.

BUKOWSKI: But I never paid so much for a car—twelve hundred dollars. One car I paid thirty-five dollars for. This was my first car, when I was with Jane. And we drove it to the racetrack. It had no springs, no brakes, nothing. Finally the reverse gear went out. Once, when we took it to the track, we turned on the lights to leave, and they wouldn't go on, so we had to drive out and look for a bump in the street. I said, "Jane, I see one, don't worry." I'd hit the bump—the lights didn't go on. Then I saw another one, and I went harder, and the lights did go on, and we felt good. Have a drink, Hank.

PIVANO: She sounds very simpatico, this girl to me.

BUKOWSKI: So I always had old cars like that, and you fall in love with those old cars, because they're not supposed to run, but they keep right on running. You learn how to do little things to them, you carry a can of something, you pull on the motor. I learned all the tricks. You just learn cars: you clean the spark plugs, you check the water, you put tape on loose wires, you do all kinds of things. Now I don't do that any more. I just get in and I drive.

WOLBERG: And then he takes it to the shop and waits a day for it.

BUKOWSKI: Right.

WOLBERG: The last time he took the BMW to the shop, he stayed in the motel to wait for it to get fixed. (laughter)

PIVANO: For a while I used to have a very small, battered car, very small one, very old, very small, but she was so dear to me. And she was so nice to me, that, whenever she broke, she broke in front of a garage. So it never, never, never gave me any preoccupation. I talked to her. I said, "Now be a kind car this time." I talked to her, like to the cat, you know. It was a living vehicle.

BUKOWSKI: Yeah, they get like that. I understand that.

PIVANO: Well, what do you think of the fact that you are more popular in Europe than in America?

BUKOWSKI: Well, I like it as a convenience, because it's over *there* that it's happening and I can go along more or less normal and live normally here, you know, not being bothered. Did you ask the reason that's happening? Or do I like it?

PIVANO: Yes. Why do you think this happened? Because you are hugely popular in Europe, as you know.

BUKOWSKI: Well, I'm going to say something dumb—I just think Europe is a couple centuries ahead of the United States. I think the people over there are more perceptive, they just know more. I guess the culture has been over there longer, they live differently and they're more perceptive. They just pick up what is real more quickly than the Americans do. That's the only thing I can think of. If I lived there, well, I couldn't walk down the street.

PIVANO: Why couldn't you walk down the street? Why?

L. LEE: He was like a rock star.

PIVANO: Sure. In Europe, he is a rock star.

BUKOWSKI: If I go to the laundromat, it's "Oh, Charles, Charles . . ." Anyplace I go—I go out to eat, I walk down the street—they follow me. This can make you feel very unnatural. It's very nice to walk around without thinking: I'm a writer, my name is Charles Bukowski, I'm a writer. It's very destructive to think that way. You just have to have this open, blank mind.

PIVANO: You know what Ginsberg says when they ask him, "Are you Mr. Ginsberg?" He says, "One of them."

BUKOWSKI: Oh, that's very good. That's great, that puts them off.

WOLBERG: Yeah, but he loves attention. He's not uncomfortable with it.

PIVANO: No, he's not as uncomfortable as you are.

BUKOWSKI: That's why he teaches and sits in coffee houses, and I don't. I find that many writers write until they become known, and then you read on the contributor's page that so-and-so now teaches writing at such-and-such university. This happens to so many of them. First they start out as writers, and then they're teaching others how to write. How can they do this thing?

PIVANO: Ginsberg teaches and writes.

BUKOWSKI: Writing is something that you don't know how to do. You sit down and it's something that happens, or it may not happen. So, how can you teach anybody how to write? It's beyond me, because you yourself don't even know if you're going to be able to. I'm always worried, well, you know, every time I go upstairs with my wine bottle. Sometimes I'll sit at that typewriter for fifteen minutes, you know. I don't go up there to write. The typewriter's up there. If it doesn't start moving, I say, well, this could be the night that I hit the dust.

PIVANO: But that's what I'm saying, that Ginsberg doesn't teach writing. He teaches the . . . somehow, the presence of the Buddhist in authors. He does it with great devotion. Very strange.

BUKOWSKI: Well, maybe he was born to be a teacher.

PIVANO: Or a Buddhist.

BUKOWSKI: Maybe he was born to be a Buddhist. That's all very fine.

PIVANO: Yes.

BUKOWSKI: That's all very fine. What he does is very fine. Let him continue doing that, I wish him plenty of luck. But just don't make me go up there. (laughter)

PIVANO: Oh, I wasn't trying to persuade you.

PIVANO: Joe told me something that I didn't know, but I should have known. That you had a—something happened in Paris on a television interview. Tell me the story, because I didn't quite understand it.

BUKOWSKI: Well, you see I was totally intoxicated, so I'll turn it over to Linda. Because I have no idea what happened.

L. LEE: Well, the show was called *Apostrophe,* and it's the number one television show in France today. It's a very popular television show on national French television. It's a literary program with a talk-show format, with a moderator and generally four or five writers and authors. Hank was invited to be the main guest of the evening.

BUKOWSKI: I didn't know.

L. LEE: . . . along with a few other people. And he'd had some wine before we got there and they provided him with two full bottles of wine while he was on the television program. They put little translator things on everybody and had translating—immediate translation.

BUKOWSKI: Well, I demanded the wine, I remember, or I wouldn't go on.

L. LEE: Yeah. So they had it for you when you came. And so he went on and it was okay in the beginning, except that Hank immediately didn't get along with the moderator, this man Bernard Pivot, who is very popular over there, and very well-liked by the conservative people. And so Hank asked him, "Well, do you want some wine?" and he was very friendly and open and this man was ". . . oh, nononono, I don't want any wine."

BUKOWSKI: I remember that I said, "You're very nervous, aren't you?"—before the program. "Why are you so nervous? What are you worried about? Here, let me pour you some wine." "Oh, no."

L. LEE: Very snotty guy. And so the evening went on, and the first thirty minutes were okay, but then Hank was becoming drunk. And he sort of took over, and Bernard Pivot didn't like that, because he wanted to have the other people talking, and so forth. And Hank didn't want that, he wanted to be the main attraction. He started making some comments about the other people there. There was one woman writer there. These people were called "marginal" writers. That was the topic of the evening.

PIVANO: Who were they?

BUKOWSKI: There was an old white-haired communist. I told him, "You look like a good boy, baby, and all that."

L. LEE: And there was the psychiatrist that gave Antonin Artaud the shock treatments that eventually destroyed him. And he was also one of the guests.

BUKOWSKI: He kept looking at me. (laughter)

PIVANO: Very strange. He was interested.

L. LEE: So the evening went on and Hank got drunk and it just got worse and worse and worse. It was a live television broadcast, and so . . .

WOLBERG: Millions of people . . .

BUKOWSKI: Oh, yes, there was the lady author there. I said, "Well, I can tell if you're a good writer or not. Lift your skirt and let me look at your legs and I'll tell you if you're a good writer or not." See, this type of thing. I remember saying that. I guess there were other rejoinders made.

L. LEE: But Hank kept talking and talking and interrupting all the other people and Bernard Pivot was getting very upset because he didn't know how to deal with him, he'd never confronted such a situation in his life, he was like a wind-up toy. And everything was supposed to be just right with the right questions asked, and the right answers given, and so forth. Hank was completely different, and so he didn't know what to do with him, and he became very embarrassed. Finally he put his hand over Hank's mouth and said, "Shut up! Shut up!" and Hank said, "Wait a minute now," and he put his hand away, and kept talking and talking and the other people were upset because they didn't get a chance to express themselves, and it went on and on and finally the moderator couldn't take it any more and he said, "That's enough, that's enough, if you don't shut up now . . ." And at that, Hank took his bottle and stood up, threw the translator piece out of his ear, threw it on the ground, took his bottle, finished the entire thing in one long gulp, and began to walk off the program.

BUKOWSKI: No one had ever walked off it . . .

L. LEE: No one had ever done this on this program. Nobody knew what to do. The audience was cheering, the people in the translator booth couldn't translate any more, they were laughing so hard, and this Bernard Pivot was just out of his mind. He was going crazy, he just didn't know how to handle it at all, and the other people were just going—"Get rid of him, so we can talk." So, we went out with an entourage of about ten people.

PIVANO: And then what happened?

BUKOWSKI: Then we got to the front door. And there were some guards, because it's government-run, so there were some military men at the door. Hank pulled his knife out and he started screaming at them, "Let me out of this fuckin' place. Now." All this, and they didn't know if he was serious or not. Then they realized he might do something, he was crazy. They lifted him up and went *whoosh*—out the front door.

PIVANO: Oh, no.

L. LEE: And everybody was taking pictures, and, oh, it was like a movie. It was like a crazy film.

PIVANO: Thank you, Linda.

L. LEE: But the next day, all the major newspapers all over France had written about this situation. And, finally, French national television had something worthwhile to look at. Charles Bukowski, our hero.

BUKOWSKI: It worked, but it was unplanned.

L. LEE: Yeah, perfect, perfect. We were walking down the street in a very expensive section of Paris and three very very upper-class women came walking down the street and one of them noticed Hank. And she said, "Oh, look," to her friends, and they were all embarrassed and they went "Ohohoh, that's Charles Bukowski, Charles Bukowski." These were the matrons, you know, and they were so excited.

PIVANO: Thank you, Linda. And what do you think of the thing, now that you've heard it told? Are you proud of yourself or what?

BUKOWSKI: Oh, I think, yeah, I like what I did. But, see, I do the same thing here almost three nights a week. With whoever's around. That's just my natural thing. I just happened to be on TV instead of sitting around here.

PIVANO: But is it because the TV excites you? Because you are being very sweet to me. You don't insult me.

BUKOWSKI: Well, you see, I haven't had much to drink yet.

PIVANO: Oh, that's the cause.

BUKOWSKI: Yeah, stick around. It just progresses gently, all of a sudden it happens. (laughter) . . .So,well, there's more to that. We went to Nice, and Linda's uncle refused to let me in the house because he'd seen me on the TV program.

L. LEE: He lives in St. Paul de Vence. And we were supposed to be going to visit with him for a few days. And Pivot was his hero. He said, "I will never let Bukowski through my door. Never."

BUKOWSKI: He let us make the trip. I didn't want to see him anyhow.

L. LEE: But we'd gone all that way to Nice for that purpose.

BUKOWSKI: But a very nice thing happened in Nice. It was the next day, we were sitting at a cafe having coffee and a waiter came up and said, "Charles Bukowski." He then waved about five other waiters over. They all lined up. That made me feel good. I thought it was one of the nicest things. It was done in style.

PIVANO: Style, yes.

BUKOWSKI: Those waiters had style. They all bowed down.

L. LEE: They didn't come over and bother him or anything. That was all, just bowed and walked off.

PIVANO: This is what Hemingway was feeling of the waiters. He appreciated them very much for the help they were giving him without intruding.

BUKOWSKI: Exactly. I felt that in Europe. I'd been warned that the waiters are bastards, they're really sons-of-bitches. But I found them completely normal, like they weren't even waiters, they were people acting as waiters. They just smiled, it was totally neat.

PIVANO: Did you ever meet Hemingway?

BUKOWSKI: No, no, we were many years apart. And I guess that when he died I hadn't even been published.

PIVANO: I think you would have liked him, he was a very generous man—very, very good man. And a very true man. You'd be surprised at how many proofs of loyalty he was giving all the time. Always toward poor people, you know. But you like his writing, don't you?

BUKOWSKI: I like it less than I used to.

PIVANO: Less now?

BUKOWSKI: Yes. His books have no sense of humor. But, I liked his lines, of course, we were all hooked on his lines.

PIVANO: Which books did you like?

BUKOWSKI: Well, his earlier books. I don't know the order of them, but I found each succeeding book a little bit worse.

PIVANO: Did you like *Farewell to Arms?*

BUKOWSKI: No.

PIVANO: No?

BUKOWSKI: Oh, wait. *Farewell to Arms* was one of the early ones, with the nurse who . . .

PIVANO: With the nurse, yes.

BUKOWSKI: And she said, "It's a dirty trick playing . . ." Yeah, that was good. And *To Have and Have Not*, what's the other one?

PIVANO: *The Sun Also Rises*.

BUKOWSKI: Yeah. I liked that. But when he'd gone up to Spain, what was it?

PIVANO: *For Whom the Bell Tolls.*

BUKOWSKI: Yeah. I didn't like that. And I didn't like *The Old Man and the Sea*, just the early ones were good.

PIVANO: But why did you like him then, and not now?

BUKOWSKI: Well, he got milky, the lines were no longer straight and strong. They became tame.

PIVANO: The late books, you mean?

BUKOWSKI: Yeah, they just became fat, they didn't have the same cleanliness to them.

PIVANO: And in the beginning you liked it because it was sharp?

BUKOWSKI: Brittle, sharp. And yet he still said things with these easy lines, which influenced me, I'm sure. Subconsciously, I try to do the same thing, say it as simply as possible and still say what is needed to be said.

PIVANO: I'm glad you said that, because I was thinking that, but I didn't dare say it.

BUKOWSKI: Keep it simple, and make it simpler yet. And then make it simpler yet. Hemingway—the line is what I pick up on, you know, the one line at a time. Hemingway. And then Saroyan had a good, easy line.

PIVANO: Saroyan, yes.

BUKOWSKI: But he had too much sugar, too many fairy tale dancers.

PIVANO: He is really a writer of the times, while Hemingway is a universal writer.

BUKOWSKI: Saroyan was very optimistic, and the optimism got a little bit sickening. I would have liked to see him get angry or depressed now and then, but still use that same easy line. And there is another. John Fante.

PIVANO: John Fante? I wouldn't think of him.

BUKOWSKI: He was, maybe, my main influence.

PIVANO: Is he?

BUKOWSKI: I always mention this in an interview, yeah. I read him when I was about eighteen and I said, "This guy can write."

PIVANO: What did you like about Fante?

BUKOWSKI: What did I like? Everything. I first read *Ask the Dust*.

PIVANO: *Ask the Dust?*

BUKOWSKI: And I liked it so much I started telling people about it, and now John Martin, my publisher, has reproduced it. I mean, he has republished *Ask the Dust*, so people are getting to read it.

PIVANO: John Martin is the editor at Black Sparrow.

BUKOWSKI: He published Fante last year. Fante is relatively unknown. He was discovered by H. L. Mencken.

PIVANO: Mencken, yes.

BUKOWSKI: Fante's a good boy. He's dying.

PIVANO: He's still living?

BUKOWSKI: Well, he has one leg chopped off and he's blind and he's dying of diabetes, very slowly.

PIVANO: Is he poor?

BUKOWSKI: He went to Hollywood and got a little money, has his own home. I don't think he has any financial concerns.

PIVANO: He gets along, but he isn't well?

BUKOWSKI: He has medical benefits and all that.

PIVANO: How old is he now? Eighty or seventy?

BUKOWSKI: Seventy.

PIVANO: Fante is translated into Italian.

BUKOWSKI: He is Italian.

PIVANO: Yes, yes, he is translated into Italian, but I wasn't connecting Fante.

WOLBERG: In Hank's *Women* or I think it's in *Women* or one of Hank's books, he wrote about—mentioned the names of people, and one of them was John Fante. And John Martin was reading it. He'd never heard of John Fante. He called Hank up and was talking to him and he said, "By the way, that name, 'John Fante,' is great. It's a great name. You've got a good sense of making up names." Hank said, "I didn't make that name up." (laughter)

PIVANO: Oh, that's incredible. Only a publisher could say something like that. Only a publisher.

WOLBERG: John Martin did read John Fante. And he said, "Yeah, is he still alive?" Anyway, this is how John Martin is now publishing John Fante.

BUKOWSKI: I have compassion, but I also have insanity. One of Fante's weaknesses is he's totally sane. There's no madness in him. You know madness is very interesting. And I like a writer to be a little bit strange, or demented—just a touch. I can have compassion, but I like a writer to be a little bit crazy as well, so I'm not quite sure what he's going to say next.

PIVANO: Yes. Unpredictable.

BUKOWSKI: When I sit down to write, I like to feel the same way. I don't know what the next line is. So you see, it gets through Fante, and Saroyan, and Hemingway, borrowing a line and then putting my own line kind of through that and using myself.

PIVANO: Something I resented very much was one day I read that you were the new Miller and the new Kerouac. This was something that I resented so much because I don't think that you have anything to do with them.

BUKOWSKI: There's no connection.

PIVANO: I really think that you are far away from their attitude, their way of living, their everything. Just because Kerouac was drinking. But, you know, there were many people who were drinking. Fitzgerald was also drinking. But you have nothing to do with Fitzgerald.

BUKOWSKI: Nothing. Well, I think that it's blurred . . .

PIVANO: . . . media image.

BUKOWSKI: Yeah, people say, "You must like Henry Miller." And I tell them that I've read a little bit of him, but I can't get into his books. He's okay when he's writing about fucking, but when he gets philosophical, I fall asleep. So I really haven't given him a fair chance. I'd just pick up a few of his paperbacks while I was bumming the country, and I used to try to read them while I was riding on the bus. And the fucking parts were great, they were very human. But then he'd get up into philosophizing and using larger language . . . I'd lose track and fall asleep on the bus.

PIVANO: You never met him?

BUKOWSKI: No.

PIVANO: He was so close.

BUKOWSKI: Should I tell her about the son?

PIVANO: The son?

BUKOWSKI: He wanted to meet me. He claimed that I was the world's greatest writer. And I said, "Look behind you while you're phoning." And he said, "Oh, no, he's done now. You're the new thing."

PIVANO: He said that about his father?

BUKOWSKI: He's dying. Well, you know about sons and fathers. When you're so close like that, you tend to overlook, so it's a natural reaction to look elsewhere.

WOLBERG: But didn't Henry Miller once write you a letter saying that he thought you were one of the greatest writers around?

BUKOWSKI: No, ah . . .

L. LEE: Miller never wrote Bukowski.

BUKOWSKI: But he did write me a letter through Martin. But something happened and it ended up with Martin sending him something, and Miller owing me money. (laughter)

PIVANO: That's good.

BUKOWSKI: I don't understand how this happened, but I got a hold of his address, and I reminded him that he owed me a certain amount of money for some reason or other. And he wrote back this letter in hand—not typewritten. But he must have heard something about me, because he went on to lecture me. He said, "You know, drinking is not good for creation. If you want to keep creating, you must stop drinking. You must give up drinking." I'm sure he did a little drinking too, I don't know.

PIVANO: It's really unbelievable that he wrote such a thing as that.

BUKOWSKI: John Martin has the letter now. He used to come over to my place and say, "You got any poems?" I'd tell him to just open the closet door. He'd open it and this big mass of sheets of paper would fall out. He used to pick these poems out and say, "I can make broadsides out of these." And so one time he saw this letter, and he said, "Gee, is this letter from Henry Miller?" I said, "Yeah, he owes me some money." He asked, "Do you mind if I take it?" I told him to go ahead. Well, I didn't realize a damn thing. He got two hundred and eighty dollars for it. But, that's okay. John helped me. He's still helping me and I'm helping him.

PIVANO: Is John Martin an author, or a publisher?

BUKOWSKI: Publisher. He never wrote a book.

PIVANO: You are going to publish your next book on your boyhood with him?

BUKOWSKI: All my books are Black Sparrow, except now and then, when Martin loses his mind, City Lights gets lucky.

WOLBERG: We get the shit.

BUKOWSKI: You get the rejects. (laughter)

PIVANO: Is it going to be a big book or small book?

71

BUKOWSKI: The way it is now, I'm up to page fifty and I'm still in about the sixth grade. So it looks like it's going to be mammoth.

PIVANO: It's going to be an autobiography?

BUKOWSKI: It's going to be like that. I don't know how they're going to publish it.

L. LEE: *Ham on Rye*—the title.

PIVANO: Ham—on . . .

L. LEE: Yeah, on rye. It's a sandwich.

PIVANO: Rye?

L. LEE: Rye bread.

BUKOWSKI: You see, you take a bite, I'm the ham.

WOLBERG: If you take *Factotum, Post Office,* and *Women,* put them together, you have pretty much an autobiography. The only thing that's missing is the early years.

BUKOWSKI: From birth to *Factotum.*

WOLBERG: So, when he finishes this book, he's got no more reason to write.

BUKOWSKI: Caught up. Finished.

PIVANO: He will find some. You will always find some. Tell me about the movies, this *Barfly*. What does *Barfly* mean?

BUKOWSKI: Well, I think it's an American expression. It's a guy who, like me in the old days, would just sit on a bar stool from the moment he woke up until the bar closed. I guess that *barfly* comes from when there are beer suds on the bar and the flies circle around, land on it, kick around and take off again. A barfly is a person who is in the bar all the time, he subsists there, he needs it. And I was a barfly for a long long time. I would just sit on a barstool. I'd go in in the morning and sit there, and maybe I'd have a dime for my first draft beer, and I'd just hope somebody would buy me a drink. I was the neighborhood character. I was this young kid who—while everybody else was trying to make money, having jobs—just sat on this bar stool. And drank and drank and drank. So the screenplay is about . . . it covers only about three or four nights. But, for me, it was about a five year period.

PIVANO: Three or four nights?

BUKOWSKI: Nights and days. Lasts about that. Maybe a little longer, I haven't figured that out.

PIVANO: And the story you tell is the story of what's going on in the bar, where the barfly is.

BUKOWSKI: What this guy does, yeah. Maybe it's longer than that. Maybe it's a week or so.

WOLBERG: There are fights, bar fights, and there's a girlfriend and another woman—a wealthier woman, who's a literary agent, a publisher or whatever and she wants to take him out of the bar and into the limelight . . . the money and fame element. There's the conflict.

PIVANO: Tell the story of the screenplay, again.

BUKOWSKI: Well, it's about this guy like me. It's not in the screenplay, but the bar opened at seven a.m., and closed at two a.m., and then opened at seven, again. It was closed for only five hours, but I would leave the bar at two a.m. and go lay down and then be back five a.m. I would go up and knock at the door when the janitor, who was a day bartender, would start mopping the floor at five a.m. His name was Jim, and he'd let me in. And all the drinks—I would get all these free drinks from five a.m. to seven a.m. He'd pour me whiskeys and all that, so I'd be quite ready when business started. It was on the house. He was a nice guy. So while he mopped, I'd sit there and we wouldn't say too much, just a few words, and he'd keep pouring, and then he'd say, "Well, Hank, I've got to charge you now, I'm opening the door." And I'd say, "Okay Jim, thank you." So, I'd just stay in the bar. The screenplay's about the experiences of a barfly—a person who lives that type of life. You see, by hiding in this bar, I didn't have to have an eight-hour job; I didn't have to drive my car to work; I didn't have to punch a time-clock; I didn't have to get involved with society. It was a good hiding place. So all I was doing was sitting there waiting for something. I really thought something thrilling would happen in that bar. But it never did. It was just very regular.

PIVANO: No stories of women?

BUKOWSKI: That bar was so bad, a woman dare not enter. Well, women would enter that bar. At their own risk.

74

BUKOWSKI: You know, please feel free to ask as many things as you want and then, you can put it together later, in any fashion you wish. The more you have, the more you'll be able to work with.

L. LEE: Feel free to ask anything, and then when you take it back, you can just do what you want.

PIVANO: You want me to send you a copy of the interview?

L. LEE: Yes. That would be wonderful.

PIVANO: I wonder what will happen with the transcription, because, you know, we are in Italy. I have my typist who knows English very well.

L. LEE: Oh, I have an Italian friend who translates a lot of things, so if I want something translated . . .

PIVANO: No, but I mostly want it to be transcribed by someone who understands English. The difficult thing is to transcribe it in English. This is always my problem with the tapes, you know. Tell me one thing. I hear that Linda calls you Hank. Why are you called Charles in the books and Hank in your private life?

BUKOWSKI: Well, you see, that goes back to the old childhood again. My parents used to call me Henry. My full name is Henry Charles Bukowski, Junior. I got very tired of Henry, you know, Henry.

PIVANO: Why did you get tired?

BUKOWSKI: Because my parents were not nice people. And when they called me by my name, I didn't want to hear it, because the only time they called me was to either come eat, or do some task, or I had done something wrong, and I was due for a beating. In other words, I got to dislike the name Henry. So when I first started writing, I thought, Henry Bukowski? There was another reason. Now, if you take Henry and put it with Bukowski, what do you get? Hen-er-y Bu-kow-ski. You see, that jumps too much. It has little curls, Henry and Bukowski, it has little curls. You know what I mean?

PIVANO: Yes

BUKOWSKI: Henry Bukowski. I thought, Henry Bukowski, that doesn't even sound right. Then I tried Charles Bukowski. Now, Charles is a straight line, and Bukowski wiggles up and down. So, one counteracts the other. I said, "Now that sounds like a writer. Charles Bukowski." So, for two reasons, I became Charles Bukowski: one, I got tired of my parents saying "Henry," and the other was purely, shall we say, phonetic. That's the word. Now, I don't like to be called Charles, either. It's okay on a written page, but to have somebody say, "Oh, Charles," I don't like that either. So I'm all mixed up, so I tell people to call me Hank. You see, it's very jumbled up. It's okay. Charles Bukowski on the written page is all right, but I don't want to be called Charles. Hank, the good guy. Hank.

L. LEE: Hey, Hank. How ya doin', Hank?

BUKOWSKI: Good old Hank.

PIVANO: Did you invent "Hank"?

BUKOWSKI: No. Oh, you see, Hank and Henry are the same thing. It's a nickname for Henry . . . Hank. It means the same thing.

WOLBERG: The other thing, too, his father's name is Henry Charles Bukowski, and when he was first published in *Portfolio* or *Story* magazine . . .

BUKOWSKI: It was when I first got published in *Story*—but then *Portfolio* took a story. It was a huge thing. It sold for ten dollars, in those days, and it had paintings in it. Each page was different, but huge, carefully printed pages. And I was in there with Henry Miller. Name them all, I was in there. I forgot the others, maybe Sartre, and probably many others. John Martin has a copy of this thing. I don't know who was in it. I don't have a copy. Anyhow, this came out and my father discovered it. I was on the bum, and came home, starving. When I unpacked, they found the magazine in one of my bottom drawers when I was out in a bar somewhere. I heard them that night saying, "You see, he writes, but he doesn't know how to take advantage—he doesn't know what to do with his writing. I know what to do with his writing." Well, evidently he did. He pointed out there was an opening in some museum for a curator.

PIVANO: Are you willing to tell me something about your method of writing? I mean, what you do when you get up in the morning. Do you go to your table to work?

BUKOWSKI: Oh, I never type in the morning. I don't get up in the morning.

PIVANO: What is your routine?

BUKOWSKI: I drink at night. I try to stay in bed until twelve o'clock, that's noon. Usually, if I have to get up earlier, I don't feel good all day. I look, if it says twelve, then I get up, and my day begins. I eat something, and then I usually run right to the racetrack after I wake up. I bet the horses, then I come back and Linda cooks something and we talk awhile, we eat, and have a few drinks, and then I go upstairs with a couple bottles and I type—starting around nine-thirty and going on until one-thirty, two, two-thirty at night. And that's it.

PIVANO: You eat only once a day?

BUKOWSKI: Twice a day. Never three times.

PIVANO: And then you type and then rewrite it?

BUKOWSKI: Yeah, lately. I used to rewrite it without drinking, to get it straight, because I was drunk when I first wrote it. Then I'd get drunk again to straighten out the part I wrote when I was sober. And it works. So, it's very nice that way. It makes it more entertaining.

PIVANO: And, how many times do you rewrite it?

BUKOWSKI: Once. Everything once, never twice. Once is too much. Twice is impossible.

PIVANO: And when you make the revision, you do it by handwriting?

BUKOWSKI: Oh, no, I just type . . . re-type the whole thing.

PIVANO: Oh, you re-type the whole thing. Hemingway used to do that. He retyped everything.

BUKOWSKI: Oh. All right. I mean, good company. (laughter)

PIVANO: Yes.

BUKOWSKI: Then, I try to get rid of it.

PIVANO: Meaning that you give it to the publisher.

BUKOWSKI: Well, with poetry, I send it to magazines. Little magazines. But you see my problem is that I write too much, and it can't all be published. Like I sent about sixty poems to a magazine, and they could only take nineteen. I was told, "I must publish other writers, also, Bukowski, because I only have forty-four pages in my magazine." That's *The Wormwood Review*. And then there's the *New York Quarterly*. I send them masses of poems; they have twenty or thirty they're holding. I write too much; the magazines can't keep up with me. It's a problem. So, I have all these excess poems just sitting in boxes. I've got to say, most of it is pretty good. (laughter) So I'm not only pro— what you call prolific, I'm prolific, prolific, prolific. I just keep writing and writing and writing and writing and writing. And it's nice, I like it.

PIVANO: So, you make up for the time that you missed.

BUKOWSKI: Right. Sitting in the bars, pretending . . .

PIVANO: I'm not speaking of the bars, but I'm speaking of the years when you weren't writing anything. I don't know.

BUKOWSKI: That was only ten years—when I stopped writing. I only stopped for ten.

PIVANO: And why did you stop?

BUKOWSKI: I wanted to drink.

PIVANO: You couldn't get the two things together back then. But, you are doing the two things together now.

BUKOWSKI: Well, I was doing much more drinking then. And I knew I wasn't quite ready to be a writer then; I hadn't lived enough.

PIVANO: You hadn't lived enough, or you hadn't read enough.

BUKOWSKI: What the hell, I'm . . . No, I read enough. What the hell can a guy nineteen years old write about? His childhood? Huh? Who wants to hear about the childhood, when you're that close to it? So, I had to go out and wait until something happened inside of me. There was no way I could kid myself that I was ready to write something down. And, I wasn't . . . I was empty.

WOLBERG: Maybe you were also afraid of success too soon.

BUKOWSKI: No, that wasn't it. But I'm lucky that it didn't happen. But I didn't consider success.

PIVANO: Are you satisfied with the success that you have now? Or did you want some other kind of success?

BUKOWSKI: This will do fine.

PIVANO: You like it as it is.

BUKOWSKI: It's okay. In fact, it should stay at about this level. If it got better, or more—if I became more famous, I don't think it would be good for me. Too heavy. This is just right.

PIVANO: Do you like the label of "expressionist" writer? Is any label possible to impose on anyone?

BUKOWSKI: Shit, I don't even know what *expressionist* means. You see, I'm not very good with words. I've been called a *beat* writer, which I know I'm not.

PIVANO: No, you have nothing to do with that. I never dreamed to say "beat."

BUKOWSKI: I don't know what the hell they're talking about, what they're trying to do.

WOLBERG: Beaten, maybe.

BUKOWSKI: Yeah, I'm a *beaten* writer.

PIVANO: But the term "expressionist" is different.

BUKOWSKI: It's kind of an old term, isn't it? I didn't know they were still using it.

PIVANO: Yes, but the attitude, the political attitude that you have towards all kinds of conformity, from a social point of view, you see, is rather fitting.

BUKOWSKI: Well, I'm a conformist and at the same time, I'm not.

PIVANO: No, you are not a conformist.

BUKOWSKI: Well, what I mean by conformist is that I'm a man that really doesn't want to be bothered by outside forces. In other words, I want to be left alone, and I think a lot of small people feel the same way. They want to do their job and come home and look at television and be quiet in their room. This is the way I conform . . . I told Linda the other day, after we came home from three days at Del Mar, I said, "I'm just a home boy; all I want to do is sit around, take off my shoes, lay down on the bed, and look at the ceiling. I don't need anything; I don't need to go anywhere." That's what I mean by conforming. I'm not an exhibitionist, and I'm not an extremist, except mentally, sometimes, I go a little bit goofy. By conformist, I mean I'm pretty common in my thought process. A drink, a good night's sleep, feed the cat, go to the track. See what I mean? In a certain sense I do conform. I don't want to blow up a bridge, or change the government. I'm not excited by those things.

PIVANO: But you said at the beginning that you couldn't stand doing what the other people are doing.

BUKOWSKI: But you see, I do it in a different way. When I sleep, they sleep. I sleep differently.

PIVANO: You do?

BUKOWSKI: Exactly so.

PIVANO: Do you feel like God?

BUKOWSKI: Well, you see, since I'm an agnostic, I can't answer that question.

PIVANO: Yes. And if you weren't an agnostic?

BUKOWSKI: I would probably feel like the Devil.

PIVANO: Yes.

BUKOWSKI: He's all red, and has his horns, and has a nice long tail.

PIVANO: You like the long tail, mostly, heh?

BUKOWSKI: The Devil is far more interesting than Christ.

PIVANO: Sure, oh, but when I say God, I don't mean Christ.

BUKOWSKI: Well, I, oh, of course, he's just an appendage, but . . .

PIVANO: Mostly because Christ has now assumed such a nineteenth-century English image, you know—with the long hair, and the sweetish face. This is not Christ.

BUKOWSKI: People often . . . they don't go to God, they go to Christ.

PIVANO: Yes, the Catholics, yes

BUKOWSKI: So it's getting very perverted.

L. LEE: Oh, yeah, the born-again Christian.

PIVANO: Yes, born again. What's the name of the book? *Born Again*. Have you ever heard Bob Dylan, do you like him? I mean his poems, not his music.

BUKOWSKI: Yes. He's only written one good poem. But even that's not very good. Something about the trees and all that.

PIVANO: Oh, you're thinking of the blown-down one.

BUKOWSKI: No, there's something about, I don't know, I've seen it published, and it's almost good, except it gets kind of weak. It drips off at the end. Dylan's words are common, but they're also very weak. In other words, there's a touch of melodrama there that doesn't quite ring true. Of course, you need this to be a popular song-writer—all the rock lyrics of the rock stars are the same way. They get up and they talk about love and life and the truth and they don't know what the hell they're talking about.

PIVANO: But in the beginning Dylan was talking about nuclear problems, and race problems, and war problems. What do you think of the nuclear problem?

84

BUKOWSKI: Nuclear problem? I don't stay awake nights worrying about it. In fact, I don't even consider it.

PIVANO: Why?

BUKOWSKI: Because I'm wondering who's going to win the second race on Tuesday, at the harness race.

PIVANO: So, you are not socially committed.

BUKOWSKI: I'm indifferent.

PIVANO: May we say that?

BUKOWSKI: I'm indifferent to the destruction of the human race; it doesn't matter to me. If they wiped out all humanity, nothing would be lost at all.

PIVANO: So you wouldn't mind if they dropped an atomic bomb?

BUKOWSKI: I would mind if I were standing nearby, you see.

L. LEE: You wouldn't have a chance to mind. It's funny, though, because San Pedro is one of the first places to get hit if anything happened because it's the largest seaport.

BUKOWSKI: Well, being selfish, I've already got sixty years in. I've already beaten the odds. No, I'm indifferent to all that. Destroy humanity, I don't care. And I don't worry about saving the whale or the great white leopard or the black panther or anything. I'm not concerned. All I want to do is walk down to the corner and buy the newspaper and read about a rape down the street or about a bank being held up and maybe go out and eat lunch somewhere and have a beer and just walk around and look at a dog or scratch myself under my arms. I'm just not concerned with the greater issues.

PIVANO: And what if a war started? What do you do? Think?

BUKOWSKI: I would think this is normal. This is no surprise.

PIVANO: But you wouldn't do anything to avoid it? If you could?

BUKOWSKI: To start it, avoid it, be in it—I'm just here—what occurs is beyond me.

PIVANO: Do you feel as if you are tired of something? Or do you feel as if you have the same energies that you had years ago?

BUKOWSKI: Actually, I have more energy now than I had when I was fifteen.

PIVANO: You have more now?

BUKOWSKI: Yeah.

PIVANO: Because success gave you energy?

BUKOWSKI: No. Not working the eight-hour job has helped to give me energy. And drinking better wine, instead of rot-gut, has given me energy.

L. LEE: Vitamins.

BUKOWSKI: Vitamins.

PIVANO: You got vitamins?

BUKOWSKI: MMM. And sleeping until noon every day, without going to a goddamned job, has given me energy. Each day of each year seems to be getting luckier. I mean, I feel better at sixty than I did at fifty. I felt better at fifty than I did at forty. I felt better at forty than I did at thirty. It seems like people try to avoid old age, it seems to me as though my energy gets better and better, and better luck.

L. LEE: Gettin' better all the time.

BUKOWSKI: It seems to be, I'm very serious. I can laugh while I'm saying it, but it seems to be very true. So it's rather nice, and I'll accept a nice thing now and then, but I won't make much of it. When I'm seventy, things will be really good.

PIVANO: Let's wait, that's a long time off. Many things could happen.

BUKOWSKI: Maybe when I get in the grave, things will be beautiful.

WOLBERG: Well, your royalties will certainly be at an all-time high.

PIVANO: Do you want to be cremated when you die?

BUKOWSKI: I don't care what happens then. They can burn me, they can slice me up, they can give my balls to science, it doesn't matter.

PIVANO: This is a big problem

BUKOWSKI: I'm gone.

L. LEE: But he wants to be buried near the racetrack.

BUKOWSKI: Oh, that's just a joke.

L. LEE: This is an old joke.

PIVANO: Yes. Why are you thinking of giving your balls? Is this the most significant part of you.

BUKOWSKI: Yes. Because, you see, when I was a guy in gym class, seventeen, you know, we'd strip down, and guys would point at the other guys, and say, "Gee, he's got a big cock, look at that." Then they'd point at me and say, "God, look at the balls on that guy." I had the biggest balls of any guy in the gym.

L. LEE: That's so macho.

BUKOWSKI: Oh, yeah. (laughter)

L. LEE: Hey, biggest balls around, huh?

BUKOWSKI: I don't know where the big balls come from.

WOLBERG: That's a sign of intelligence.

BUKOWSKI: Bullshit. That's a sign that maybe you have a lot of sperm. Well, I know I used to have sperm life. When I picked up Jane that first night, well, I hadn't had a woman in—how many years? So, when we went to bed, I screwed her once and ejaculated. And then I started all over, and I ejaculated again. I was going a third time, and I looked down, and she was starting to cry. I asked, "What's the matter?" She said, "God, it's endless." I said, "Oh, okay." I rolled off. So the big balls did mean something. (laughter) Every time I take a shit and flush it all down, I take another one. You've never known that, have you?

L. LEE: Oh, I figured something must have been going on.

BUKOWSKI: That stinky smell in there is pretty strange.

L. LEE: Oh, it wasn't the sperm, that's not what I smelled.

BUKOWSKI: Okay.

WOLBERG: Want to start a sperm bank, Hank? As a tax write-off?

BUKOWSKI: Yeah, it's a tax write-off.

L. LEE: Bank of Bukowski —

PIVANO: How many books have you written now? Twenty, twenty-five?

BUKOWSKI: I don't know, you know, it's just writing, writing, writing, writing, and . . . I don't count them, you know, I have no idea.

PIVANO: Do you know, Linda?

L. LEE: Well, it's not a matter of books, there are so many other things, little publications and so forth. Books, maybe fifteen.

WOLBERG: When he first started writing, he had cartons of poetry. Cartons and boxes of poems.

L. LEE: He's still doing that.

BUKOWSKI: Linda saw one of them come back the other day.

L. LEE: He still gets rejections.

PIVANO: Now?

L. LEE: Well, he sends so many, that even though they love them all, they can't print them because they have no room.

BUKOWSKI: I sent a hundred poems to a magazine. This guy said, "You know, this magazine only has forty-four pages. I've got to publish somebody else." So, he takes nineteen and tells me that he would have liked to have accepted them all but can't. "I would have liked to publish over half of what you've written, but I can't do it."

PIVANO: But do you—did you keep the things that you wrote years ago? Before you were published? Or did you throw things away?

90

BUKOWSKI: No, I threw it all away. And John Martin said, "God, why did you do that?"

PIVANO: That's too bad.

BUKOWSKI: Oh, I'm sure there was some good stuff there, but I'm sure there was an awful lot of bad stuff, too.

PIVANO: Even if you think that you have more energy now, it would be interesting to see what you had written when you were a boy.

L. LEE: Oh, there's things that he did in school. There's the one that you did when you were a young boy, that your teacher really loved.

BUKOWSKI: Oh, that's in the novel, I can't talk about it.

L. LEE: Oh, God, that's such a beautiful story.

BUKOWSKI: Well, anyhow, people ask me when I first started writing, so I can tell it now. I think I was in junior high school—the first grade of junior high, so it fits in with Hoover, you see. We had a president called Herbert Hoover, who was coming to the coliseum to visit us. My teacher said that the next assignment for the class was to go see our President and write about him and what happened. I didn't go because, you know, who cares about our President? And so, I just made the whole thing up. I wasn't even there. I wrote how his car entered the coliseum and he had garlands on and was followed by other cars, and the people stood up to see the President's face. I don't know what I said, but it was total bullshit. And it went on and on with this bullshit. Prolific, you know. So I just turned it in, and the teacher said, "Class, I want to read you something. We all had this assignment and Henry"—they called me that—"Henry has written us." She stood up and said, "I want to read this to you." It was supposed to be good writing, you know, but it was a pack of lies. I wasn't even there.

L. LEE: And it was the best story.

BUKOWSKI: They didn't even know it, or so I thought. But you see I don't write that way now. I tell mostly what occurs, but back then, the lie really worked.

L. LEE: Yeah.

BUKOWSKI: So that was the first recognition. When the teacher stood up, I said, "Oh-oh." I thought, *something's happening here.* When I went to college we had an assignment one time—city college—to turn in at least one essay a week. So, finally, at mid-term, she went down the seats: "McDonald, none. Thomas, one. Smith, two, Bukowski, forty-seven." Oh, shit. She said they were all excellent. And then I thought, *Holy Christ, I must have something going here.* Because it's so easy to do. So I always felt, early on, that there was something working, somewhere. But I still took ten years off. So, it's just like you plant a seed of corn in the ground, here comes the tree.

L. LEE: A tree? That has the corn?

BUKOWSKI: So I bring you corn.

PIVANO: When did you decide to become a writer? When your teacher said that you were good?

92

BUKOWSKI: Uh-huh. I forgot all about that. I decided to become a writer when I started reading the *Atlantic Monthly* and *Harper's*—two magazines with supposedly good writing. *The New Yorker* too. I would read these short stories they'd publish and they were absolutely nothing. They said nothing, they did nothing, they . . .

PIVANO: John Updike.

BUKOWSKI: Yes, I include him. And they were terrible, they just bored me. There was no life to them, and yet, these people were getting famous writing these stories, and I thought, I know their secret: They try to write about nothing at all, in the most boring way possible. No, I really felt that. I said, this must be some kind of snob inner circle secret. I must write something very boring that says nothing at all for pages and pages, and say it so boring that everybody gets bored. Then you think, this is really good writing, because I'm so bored, and nothing is said. So I tried the other way, I tried to say: A guy comes home from work, his wife screams at him, and he murders her. Like, a factory worker. They didn't want that. So . . .

PIVANO: They? Who are they?

BUKOWSKI: The editors. I don't know, I guess I became a writer, not so much because I thought I could be a writer, but because all the known writers that were famous seemed to me to be so very bad. But for me to just stop and let them take over with their dull badness seemed to be an atrocity. So I started typing, trying to say it the way I thought it should be said—what was happening, but in a simple way.

PIVANO: This is true of Hemingway. He remembers to say the simple thing.

BUKOWSKI: Oh, yes. Hemingway was worried about war, and bravery, and . . .

PIVANO: About death.

BUKOWSKI: And death, that's okay, but I was thinking about the simple man who went to work every day.

PIVANO: Oh, yes, I understand.

BUKOWSKI: Hemingway can have his wars, and his bravery. I have the other things that were happening to me and to everybody around me. Millions of guys and women going mad and being murdered inch by inch, every day. That was the real world. That was the death.

PIVANO: Yes. So right.

BUKOWSKI: Yeah. Because it was happening to me, I recognized it, and too often a guy would say to me, "Bukowski, we're going to let you go." Why? Not because I didn't do my work, but because I did. But I acted like I didn't enjoy doing my work. I worked hard. Sometimes I slacked, depending upon conditions, but I could work hard, and often I did. I always did it with a certain sneer or scowl, like I couldn't stand it. I didn't appreciate every tiny little salary.

PIVANO: Yes, they expect you also to be happy. Not only grateful, but also happy.

BUKOWSKI: Yes, on a small, non-livable salary. And many of them pretended to be happy. "Oh, good morning, Mr. —." I could never say, "Oh, good morning, Mr. —." I was always getting fired. Or, I was quitting. If I didn't get fired, I'd quit. You know, if I was in a place three weeks, I'd say, "This is happening too long. I haven't been fired yet."

PIVANO: But how could you have so many jobs and get fired if you worked so long for the post office.

BUKOWSKI: Let's see, this came toward the end.

PIVANO: Oh, there's more?

BUKOWSKI: Yeah, you see, I quit the post office ten years ago, when I was fifty years old. I started when I was thirty-nine. That makes eleven years.

PIVANO: Eleven years. And you worked other jobs before that?

BUKOWSKI: Back and forth, all the small jobs, the hundred jobs, except once again I worked for the post office, except this time I carried mail on my back. That was for two and a half years.

PIVANO: And this was after?

BUKOWSKI: No, this was before. The last one was the eleven years, from thirty-nine to fifty. Then I decided to become a professional writer. A professional writer is one who paces himself, feeds himself, has wine, puts gas in his car, feeds the cat, then goes to a movie. He gets paid for typing. I was frightened, the first week was terrible. I mean, I thought the walls of my apartment would collapse while I was sleeping—come down on my head.

PIVANO: Is that while you were writing *Post Office?*

BUKOWSKI: Well, I think I waited about a week. That first week was not only terrible, people would come around. They'd known what I'd done, and they made it worse. My landlady said, "You're crazy, man. You gave up a lifetime profession?" She'd leave and I'd go back and say, "Geez, maybe I am crazy. What have I done?" Then John Webb's son, the guy who printed my early books, was coming around drinking, that first week after I'd quit. He messed me all up. He came over and talked a lot of shit, and he had this human heart in a jar. And he'd say, "Well, you quit the post office, Bukowski, you're going to need this thing around." He pulled out a jar and I said, "What's that?" He said, "It's a human heart. I stole it from the laboratory. I've got a nurse girlfriend."

L. LEE: Oh, no. He gave you a heart in formaldehyde?

BUKOWSKI: Yeah. And I said, "Jesus, put that in the closet. We could get put in jail for this, you fool." And he says, "Yes, but nobody will know we have this human heart. Nobody." I told him, "It makes me puke. Put it away." Well, that was my first week as a professional writer. I had a human heart in my closet.

L. LEE: Ugh.

BUKOWSKI: I'd get up in the morning after drinking all night, and I'd open that door and look at the human heart. You know, it has large veins and it looks like . . . So I'd look at it and I'd run and puke up the beer. I'd go BLAUAAGH. That was a beautiful puke.

L. LEE: Ugh.

BUKOWSKI: The human heart gave me heart.

L. LEE: I've never heard that.

BUKOWSKI: Well, there are certain things that you haven't heard. I've never written about it, you see.

L. LEE: Have you heard that one, Joe?

WOLBERG: I've never heard that.

BUKOWSKI: Stick around, you'll hear—see, these guys have heard so many of my interviews.

L. LEE: Yes, but that's a new one. You have an original.

PIVANO: Why didn't you want to come to Italy, by the way? I mean, the Roman people asked you to come and you didn't want to come. Why?

BUKOWSKI: Tell them they throw too many bombs. I'm not a terrorist, no, I'm an anarchist, pacifist, and anti-nuclear. I have no politics, but they don't care.

PIVANO: They are just throwing them. You never know if it's the right-wing or the left-wing.

BUKOWSKI: Well, it's gotten to be quite a game. They each take credit, I guess, every time something happens.

L. LEE: Well, that was a good excuse for Hank not to go.

BUKOWSKI: I don't like to travel. So I told them, you know, they're bombing everybody. Then we were given a chance for a trip to Scandinavia in November. I said, "No, Linda, it's too cold."

L. LEE: And I'm terrified of airplanes.

PIVANO: I would ask them to invite you again next year, but if you don't . . .

BUKOWSKI: I hate travel.

PIVANO: Now that I know that you don't want to come, I will tell them not to ask you. They feel sorry if you say "no." It is better that they don't ask.

L. LEE: He really doesn't like to travel.

BUKOWSKI: I hate it, because I don't have my racetrack. I'm a homeboy, like I say, I just like to hang around.

PIVANO: Do you know anything at all about Italian literature? Have you ever read any Italian writer?

BUKOWSKI: Yeah. There was a guy that bought the camera—
Pirandello.

PIVANO: Oh, Pirandello, yes.

BUKOWSKI: He wrote plays, right?

PIVANO: Yes.

BUKOWSKI: Yeah, I liked his plays, some of them.

PIVANO: He had an identity problem.

BUKOWSKI: Well, I don't know. I just read it and maybe I didn't know quite what he was writing about. But I did like Pirandello. And there was Silone.

PIVANO: Oh, yes, Silone, yes.

BUKOWSKI: Yeah. He was a little political, wasn't he?

PIVANO: Yes.

BUKOWSKI: But I liked his writing style. He wrote pretty well— at least he came through in translation.

PIVANO: Thank you. Yes, he had no problem for style, you know; he had a problem for content. So, it was easy. Thank you.

BUKOWSKI: That's about all—Pirandello and Silone.

PIVANO: You never heard of a man called Pasolini?

BUKOWSKI: No.

PIVANO: The filmmaker, yes, and also a writer. He wrote beautiful poems.

L. LEE: Were his poems translated?

PIVANO: Pasolini's? I think so. But he was mostly a fiction writer. He wrote some poems, but he was mostly a fiction writer.

WOLBERG: He's an expressionist, isn't he?

PIVANO: No, he's a communist. (laughter) He was a very strict communist, very strict—an ideologist. And then at the end, he did a lot of philosophy of his own, which was very interesting in this moment of general corruption of ideas, of manners, you know, of life, because Italy is really a disaster, really a disaster.

BUKOWSKI: There was an article in the paper today about the seventy-two year old fellow who—what's his name?—Marom Morav?

PIVANO: Moravia, yes. What happened?

BUKOWSKI: Yes. I guess I wouldn't like his writing—it's politically tuned, you know. But his answers to the questions were very good and reminded me of the same answers I'd have given the lady if she were asking me those questions. You should read that. He would say, "Well, I'm really indifferent to this; I care for it, but it doesn't matter that much." You see, I like the way he answered his questions.

PIVANO: He is very intelligent, very brilliant.

WOLBERG: I would have tricked him into artificial concerns.

BUKOWSKI: His answers to the questions were very real for a seventy-two year old guy. He talked common sense. He wasn't trapped into saying something grand or unusual.

WOLBERG: But, if you'd thrown him a little bait . . .

BUKOWSKI: He avoided the bait. He just said exactly what he thought, and that's very good. You should read it. It's in today's paper. Upstairs.

PIVANO: And what American authors do you like? The classical, not the modern ones. Are there any, like Melville, you like?

BUKOWSKI: Oh, that's a tough question. No, nononono, I can't. No, I'm sorry. One is a homosexual, Walt Whitman, he was pretty good. But I wasn't exceptionally interested, it was just interesting. His energy kept things moving. But I get a little sleepy reading those long lines. But that's the only one, Walt Whitman.

PIVANO: Do you like him for his lines? Or for his conception of the ego? You know—his way of putting himself at the center of the universe. "I will sing myself."

BUKOWSKI: Oh, well, that song. That's a song, poem. That was very good. I think most of all I like that one. *The Song of Myself.*

PIVANO: You identify with that of putting yourself at the center? Explain.

BUKOWSKI: Yeah, well, you start with yourself and then, if you have anything left over, then you can take care of that. But take care of business at home, first. Then look around. You know, maybe you should feed the cat.

PIVANO: Yes.

BUKOWSKI: So, yeah, I liked his ego.

BUKOWSKI: Look at those green shoes.

L. LEE: Aren't they gorgeous? I want them. I love them.

PIVANO: You give me the size. Draw the foot on a piece of paper.

L. LEE: Hank, look, they're very comfortable.

PIVANO: Yes, they're like a glove.

L. LEE: Fantastic. Italian shoes are the best.

PIVANO: They are. They cost twenty dollars.

L. LEE: Is that right?

BUKOWSKI: I like the color.

L. LEE: Love the color.

PIVANO: And they make them for men, also, if you want them. They make them green, red, and yellow.

WOLBERG: I can see Hank in a pair of red shoes.

PIVANO: You want me to draw them right here?

WOLBERG: He doesn't need anything.

L. LEE: He needs some shoes that are comfortable.

BUKOWSKI: No, no. That would make me fight everyone. In the streets. I couldn't walk down the street.

PIVANO: Ah, you don't have this worry. You want me to try to draw your foot?

L. LEE: Sure. Okay, absolutely.

PIVANO: Maybe they're finished with these shoes, you know. We are at the end of the season.

L. LEE: I remember doing this as a child. Drawing the foot and the hand in school.

BUKOWSKI: Wasn't that fun?

L. LEE: Yes.

WOLBERG: I want to ask you a question now. About Bukowski.

PIVANO: To me? What?

WOLBERG: Did he turn out to be what you thought?

PIVANO: No. Completely different. I thought that you'd be aggressive.

L. LEE: You haven't been here long enough.

PIVANO: From your books, I thought that you were aggressive. And, instead, you are very tolerant. And it is a beautiful surprise I have. I'm very happy. This puts me—really, on the trail of your friends.

BUKOWSKI: All right. Thank you.

PIVANO: Well, thank you for being as you are.

BUKOWSKI: All right. Too bad you can't stay.

L. LEE: I know, that's what I'm thinking.

PIVANO: I had the honor and the chance of being a friend of Hemingway's, and I hope very much to be a friend of yours. But it was too short, you see. Maybe Joe will bring me again when I come to San Francisco next time.

WOLBERG: If you come back at a time when the store's not busy, then I can take you. Like this, it was very lucky that I could get away for one day, because it's so busy now.

PIVANO: The next time, I won't have to worry about the recorder. We can just spend a couple of hours together, just talking. I cannot say drinking, because I drink only soda. When he found out I wasn't drinking, Hemingway said, "Daughter, you shouldn't do that to me." He was desperate.

BUKOWSKI: Yeah, well, a person, when he drinks, likes the other person to drink with him.

PIVANO: Yes, I know. It's the same way with acid, you know.

BUKOWSKI: Oh, yeah—coke.

PIVANO: You know, if you don't do it, if you don't share it, the other people get embarrassed.

BUKOWSKI: Yes, I know.

Linda Lee at the interview, 1980.

Photo: Joe Wolberg

4
INTERVIEW (1984)

Interview with Charles Bukowski
San Pedro California
April 14, 1984
Fernanda Pivano

FERNANDO PIVANO: Would you like to talk about politics?

CHARLES BUKOWSKI: Politics? No. It's like quicksand, you see,
and when you get involved in the quicksand you can't get out
of it. Discussing politics is like discussing religion. One says
there is a God, the other says there isn't. In politics, one
believes this, the other believes that. It gets very confusing,
very ugly, very misleading, and people start screaming at each
other. They each believe in different things and it leads
nowhere. It's a waste. Of course, I know the people in control,
control all of us, I understand that, but I still can't get anywhere discussing it. (To Fernanda, who is writing): What are
you doing? Writing me a letter?

PIVANO: Yes. So, if you answer me, I will have a correspondence
with you. And then I will not know what to do with it, because

I will not be able to publish it. (They laugh) Since I met you last time you've published two books, *Ham on Rye* and this collection of short stories. You have more coming up?

BUKOWSKI: Yes, a book of poems. This summer. It's called *War All the Time.* That refers to everything, life in general— and all embracing title. I hate to get out of bed in the morning. I stay in bed for another fifteen minutes, with the covers over my face, because when I get out of bed I am going to war. And I might be killed, I might live, or I might die just a little bit that day, instead of all at once. So, it's all very difficult, but very interesting. Sometimes not even very interesting, just difficult.

PIVANO: Tell me something about *Ham on Rye* and the short stories. What was the reception to those two books?

BUKOWSKI: Well, of course, John Martin, who is not just my publisher, but also my good friend, always sends me only the good reviews. So I really don't know. I don't read everything. I rather enjoy the bad reviews, they make me laugh. When people hate me or don't understand me it kinda cheers me up. It really does. It's strange.

PIVANO: In *Ham on Rye*, you wanted to tell your boyhood life.

BUKOWSKI: I told the first things I remember, and then I took that up to the bombing of Pearl Harbor.

PIVANO: Why did you choose that?

BUKOWSKI: It seemed a good place. I had evolved into a man, and there was the war, and that makes another type of thing, and the war was another circumstance.

108

PIVANO: And the short stories? Are they the ones published in magazines?

BUKOWSKI: You see, there are some old stories out of old newspapers, and some new ones . . . mixed together.

PIVANO: And how do you recognize which are old and which are new?

BUKOWSKI: You won't know. Only I will know.

PIVANO: Why didn't you want to give the dates?

BUKOWSKI: It's not necessary. There is no need.

PIVANO: This is not so. There is a need.

BUKOWSKI: What is the need? A good story is a good story, it's immortal.

PIVANO: Because your way of writing changes with time.

BUKOWSKI: Just a little bit, not very much. I write the same now as I did ten, fifteen years ago. I just have more experience. If there is any change, I would say that a little more love, a little more kindness, have entered my stories. But I'll get rid of that stuff, perhaps. (laughter) People never know when they talk to me, whether I am serious or not. I like it better that way.

PIVANO: Tell me the story of your beautiful white cat. What happened?

BUKOWSKI: Oh, well, quickly, he was a bum, he came to the door, he was very mixed up, very unhappy. And we took him in, and he became the star, the hero of the whole house. We gave him a lot of love, a lot of attention. But when he came, he was almost finished. He had maybe 3 or 4 years to live. He had been shot, his back had been hurt once before. While he was here, a car ran him over, and I stayed with that cat for a week and a half, lying on the floor of the bathroom. The veterinarian said he'd never walk again, but I didn't believe him. And finally one day, as I watched him day by day, he got up on his front legs, dragged his bottom part. I talked to him, I didn't even go to the track. I don't want to make a long story. You shouldn't ask me about the cat, I can go on for hours. Finally he stood up on all fours, and I knew he'd had it. But he lasted a long time— after he was run over by that car. That cat had a soul. Cross eyes, shot and broken back—twice . . .

PIVANO: What did you say about putting the fan on him?

BUKOWSKI: He caught pneumonia, it was very hot, and I put the fan next to him to freshen him up, and it could have caused a chill. I hope not, but there is no way of knowing. So, he's gone, and in my next book there are two poems on him. The other cat is nice, but not quite like him.

PIVANO: Will you have another cat?

BUKOWSKI: No, there will never be another Mensch.

PIVANO: Let's talk about the Nobel Prize. Who do you think should win the Nobel?

BUKOWSKI: Do you know? I find it difficult to read anybody. So I don't know. I pick up a book and I can't read it.

PIVANO: Which book?

BUKOWSKI: Any book. I have a problem with reading writers. The best thing I want to do is read the newspaper. I read who won the baseball game, who won the last race, who was murdered, who was raped, who is in jail. But to read a book is very hard for me, because it's not interesting. For me. So whoever wins the prize—it's good. It's all right with me. I would never give a prize.

PIVANO: You never received any prize?

BUKOWSKI: Yes, I did, the Outsider of the Year, in 1963. The editor of the magazine called *The Outsider* one year decided that each year he would give an award for "outsider of the year." So, that first year he gave it to me. I won that and then he couldn't find anybody after me. That's all I have ever gotten.

PIVANO: This was for poetry?

BUKOWSKI: Well, I was writing mostly poetry for various magazines. And that editor told me one night, "Hank, you have ruined poetry for me, because after reading your poems, I can't read anybody else's." I said, "I have the same problem." This is a very serious conversation.

PIVANO: And is there any important change that has happened in your life since I last saw you?

BUKOWSKI: Everything is the same, I have just gotten a little older. I can't die just now. Oh, the cat died. Yes.

PIVANO: Why don't you ask yourself a question?

BUKOWSKI: I can never do that. I need to be asked. I don't know what's inside of me until somebody asks, otherwise I just sit all the time.

PIVANO: You didn't find any new writer? You still cling to John Fante and Hemingway?

BUKOWSKI: John Fante. I am disillusioned with Hemingway.

PIVANO: Why?

BUKOWSKI: Well, to begin with, he had no sense of humor. He also did not gamble in his writing, he didn't take chances, and he didn't invent.

PIVANO: What do you mean he didn't invent?

BUKOWSKI: I think his stuff was mostly taken from actuality. In other words, there wasn't much fiction in his stories. I think it's interesting now and then to make something up, just for the hell of it. I like his lines, his even, hard lines. Especially in the beginning. So, we all owe him a debt there. He taught us a few things about the simple thought. But still, that was it. No humor, no inventiveness. I said that, didn't I?

PIVANO: It's too bad that you never met him.

BUKOWSKI: We could have gotten drunk together.

PIVANO: You could have talked together.

BUKOWSKI: Well, we'd get drunk and then talk. Yes. But just to talk.

PIVANO: He would have told you about his travels and about his women. And then you would have talked to him about your women.

BUKOWSKI: No, I wouldn't have. I would have listened. Maybe after I had enough to drink, I would say, "Yes, she was really a bitch."

PIVANO: I hadn't prepared any questions this time.

BUKOWSKI: I hadn't prepared any answers.

PIVANO: Do you still work in the garden?

BUKOWSKI: What garden?

PIVANO: Your garden . . . there. You don't call it a garden?

BUKOWSKI: I never go out there. The only time I go out there is to get the mail . . . I go past it.

PIVANO: Linda, is it true?

LINDA LEE BEIGHLE: No, it's not true. He goes there. He was there just a little while ago.

BUKOWSKI: What? To get the garbage out?

L. LEE: No, you turn the sprinklers on, you plant some flowers.

BUKOWSKI: Oh, once in awhile I do that, but never for too long. I don't have time—the horses, the writing, drinking, sleeping, eating, and Linda take it all.

PIVANO: Do you ever go the that Vietnamese restaurant?

BUKOWSKI: No, it got bad. It changed owners.

PIVANO: And where do you go now?

BUKOWSKI: It's hard to find a place, especially in San Pedro, there aren't any eating places in this town. There is an Italian place that isn't bad.

L. LEE: Yeah. We should go. It's called La Griglia, they have excellent fresh fish. They are all Italian.

PIVANO: Next time you take me there.

BUKOWSKI: All right, if I am still alive next time. I can't die yet.

PIVANO: Please don't talk about dying.

BUKOWSKI: I drink too much, it kills all the germs.

PIVANO: We might suggest it as a good cure against cancer. What do you think?

BUKOWSKI: A good cure against cancer? I think its a cure for unhappiness. But I have to have a certain amount of unhappiness.

114

PIVANO: To be able to write . . .

BUKOWSKI: To be able to be human.

PIVANO: And to be able to be human means also to be able to write?

BUKOWSKI: To be able to write means to be inhuman. Writers aren't very nice people.

PIVANO: Explain that.

BUKOWSKI: I never met anyone I liked. I never met a garage mechanic whom I liked. Most people just aren't grade "A," meaning the best in class. You go to the dentist, he pulls the wrong tooth. You take your car to the mechanic, he can't fix it. You go to the doctor, he gives you a pill and charges you. You bet on a horse, the jockey falls off. Very few people can do what they are supposed to do.

PIVANO: What does this have to do with being inhuman?

BUKOWSKI: Well, you'd like a human to be a human. Somebody you can talk to, who will do what they say they will do. When I talk about a human, I am talking about the dream idea of the good person, someone you can trust, someone who can make you laugh, someone who is sensible and good. There don't seem to be many of these. On the freeways, in the theatres, at the markets. Maybe you and I travel different places. Maybe you meet different people. I am just saying what I have seen. I am discouraged with humanity. I like cats, dogs, elephants, tiger, spiders. No, I don't like spiders.

L. LEE: Your father liked spiders.

BUKOWSKI: My father liked everything I didn't like. He did like spiders. How do you know?

L. LEE: I read one of your poems.

BUKOWSKI: "The Spider Man!"

PIVANO: You ever been analyzed?

BUKOWSKI: I wouldn't let them.

PIVANO: Why?

BUKOWSKI: Because they might take away my good luck.

PIVANO: Why?

BUKOWSKI: Because they'd make me normal and like them. Then I couldn't write, I couldn't sleep, I would eat the wrong food, I would crash on the freeway, I would commit suicide, I would murder somebody—if someone analyzed me. This way, I am harmless. They might be wrong when they analyzed me.

PIVANO: Have you read any book of . . .

BUKOWSKI: Freud? All that stuff?

PIVANO: No, I was thinking more of the Americans, like Erikson.

BUKOWSKI: A psychologist?

PIVANO: His stories are extraordinary—like Mark Twain's, frontier like.

BUKOWSKI: I didn't like Mark Twain.

PIVANO: You didn't? Erikson was living in Arizona, in Phoenix, and these stories . . .

BUKOWSKI: I don't like Phoenix.

PIVANO: Oh, god! Come on, what do you mean? You sabotage! Don't do this to me!

BUKOWSKI: I don't do it to you . . .

PIVANO: I'm a good girl; I bring you Easter lilies.

BUKOWSKI: I appreciate that. That has nothing to do with the other things.

PIVANO: Erikson was good. And there was another one, also American. Helmut Burgler, who tried to analyze writers' blocks.

BUKOWSKI: I don't have blocks.

PIVANO: I know, we are not speaking of you. We are talking about writers who have blocks.

BUKOWSKI: Okay, thank you.

PIVANO: Sometimes it happens. There are those who analyze blocks.

BUKOWSKI: Oh, I know what causes a block.

PIVANO: What causes a block?

BUKOWSKI: You are not living the way you should live.

PIVANO: For instance? What might cause a block to you? If you couldn't go to the horse track?

BUKOWSKI: Well, now, if I had a broken leg, or if somebody told me I couldn't go, yes, that would cause a block.

PIVANO: A broken leg!

BUKOWSKI: You caught me there. No, if for some reason I couldn't go, I probably still wouldn't get a block, I think . . . People get into unnatural situations. Say, they make too much money, and this makes them live a different way. They buy a BMW, an electric typewriter, a copying machine, a swimming pool . . .

PIVANO: Did you buy a swimming pool?

BUKOWSKI: I fought very hard against it. I didn't want it because everybody would be in it but me: the neighbors, their children, everybody I dislike would be out there splashing around. I'd be sitting in here just like I am now. Swimming pools are not for me. That would cause a block. You must not be guided by other people's ideas or ways. They get in the way of your own. You must be selfish with your happiness.

PIVANO: That is very lovely.

BUKOWSKI: Yeah, I like that too.

PIVANO: And what are your plans for the future? What are you going to write now that you've finished your book of poems?

BUKOWSKI: There are always more poems, more short stories. They come by themselves.

PIVANO: And the short stories you're writing are for which magazines?

BUKOWSKI: *Oui* and *High Times*. Once a month I have a regular column.

PIVANO: But you are not planning a new novel?

BUKOWSKI: No. I started three of them, and in each one the beginning was good, then I found myself forcing the writing. So I said, "no." When it becomes work for the writer, it is work for the reader. They feel the lack of joy, the lack of dash.

PIVANO: So you stopped them.

BUKOWSKI: Yes.

5
NOTES

The year 1966 marked the beginning of Bukowski's professional life with John Martin's Black Sparrow Press. Then, in 1969, Doug Blazek published a small collection of poems and short stories, *A Bukowski Sampler,* some of which was to appear again later in Black Sparrow's seminal *Burning in Water, Drowning in Flame.* In that same year, Essex House published a collection of Bukowski's work that had already appeared in *Open City.* It bore the same title as his column: *Notes of a Dirty Old Man.* (This collection later [1973] marked his entrance into the writer's gallery of Lawrence Ferlinghetti's "City Lights Books.")

The critical establishment gave Bukowski's *Notes of a Dirty Old Man* and other writings a cold reception, so they collapsed in silence. But Bukowski already had his audience. It was growing in numbers. It flocked to his poetry readings—not just to see the poet but to see the "cursed poet," the man who was always drunk, had to be pushed onstage, was seduced by young girls, students, and women 20 or 30 years younger than himself. Bukowski made no refutation. He liked to project himself as an indefatigable lover.

Even if *Notes of a Dirty Old Man* sometimes recalls the false ingenuousness of Saroyan, and has irritatingly precious and artificial punctuation, a la e. e. cummings and other writers of the avant-garde 1920s, it has in embryo many of the qualities that appear later.

As a craftsman striving to master the trade, Bukowski came to refine his style, make wiser use of salacious language, and develop an extraordinary skill in dialogue that immediately lifted it to the level of Hemingway. He mixes in a type of humor that is as self-destructive as Norman Mailer's, as caustic as that of John Fante. Only someone who had known years of living on survival's edge could have brought these qualities to his work.

Notes of a Dirty Old Man

The stories in *Notes of a Dirty Old Man* changed scenery from Kansas City to Philadelphia, from Atlanta to Texas, from New Orleans to New York; and the pages are full of names loved by his audience of the time: Neal Cassady, William Burroughs, Barney Rosset, and Taylor Meade. Bukowski sometimes calls himself by his real name, sometimes as "Stirkoff" or others.

Between a fuck and a horse race, a puke and a crap, Bukowski enunciated his appraisals of the literary world:

"Outside of Dreiser, T. Wolfe was the worst American writer ever born."

"I was a student of Dostoevski and listened to Mahler in the dark."

"Burroughs is a very dull writer."

"Faulkner is nothing."

He gives his thoughts on how to write about sex. There's an essay on it in the middle pages.

"sex is interesting but not totally important. I mean, it's not even as important physically as excretion."

Continuing to use lower case, he goes on with a revealing statement:

122

"sex is obviously a tragicomedy. I don't write about it as an instrument of obsession. I write about it as a stage play laugh where you have to cry about it, a bit, between acts. Giovanni Boccaccio wrote it much better. he had the distance and the style. I am still too near the target to effect total grace. people simply think I'm dirty. if you haven't read Boccaccio, do. you might begin with *The Decameron*."

He comments about his own sexuality: ". . . I still have a little distance and after 2,000 pieces of ass, most of them not very good, I am still able to laugh at myself and my trap."

If you can get beyond the passe punctuation—an expression one gathers, stemming mostly from rebellion to the norm—you'll find in *Notes of a Dirty Old Man* the key to understanding his next books. You'll also unlock the phenomenon of alcoholism that has wasted him and soaks his pages:

"I can't tell you why I had to drink so much. maybe for my great anger or for my great grief, or because I was missing a piece of my brain-soul. or maybe for both things."

The roots of Bukowski's way with humor is also planted in *Notes of a Dirty Old Man*. Bukowski sees himself as a robot thrown from one woman to another, pushed away by their whims and curiosities, dominated by their will-power:

"Women never let us sleep until we are dead."

"It's not me that leaves women, they leave me."

"She said she wouldn't go to bed with me until we got married. so we got some sleep and I drove all the way to Vegas and back, we were married."

". . . the underbelly of Texas and her crazy women with tricks that won't turn who cry and fuck you, leave you, write homey letters every Christmas, even tho you are now a stranger, won't let you forget . . ."

There are many more examples.

Post Office

In 1971, two years after publication of the poetry collection, *The Days Run Away Like Wild Horses Over the Hills*, his first novel was published. This was *Post Office*. It was clean of affected style and solidified his Hemingwayesque manner. The book strikes a classic chord, founded as it is on the Hemingway approach. Bukowski said it took 19 days to write—at least that's what he claimed. It tells about the three and a half years he spent as a mailman and the 11 years he spent as a postal clerk. The *Times Literary Supplement* wrote that *Post Office* was "comical, cruel, cynical, pitiless and self-ironic."

In *Post Office* Bukowski certainly shows no mercy for himself or others. In it, Bukowski takes the name of "Henry Chinaski"—a name he will keep for all his next works—and recounts the adventures of a mailman. A dog bites him. A woman lets him rape her. A truck sinks in a flood. And so on.

He also tells two true and important love stories. One of them is the story of "Betty," divorced from a wealthy man, now squandering her money on riotous living, and ending in an alcoholic death. The other story concerns "Joyce," a Texan nymphomaniac multimillionaire, who marries him and then dumps him in favor of "the guy with the purple stick-pin." There is also the true tale of "Fay," who gave Bukowski a daughter. Of lesser importance is the account of a mulatto woman, "Vi," and other stories, such as the one where a medical student gives him a human heart preserved by formaldehyde in a glass jar, and Bukowski panics and puts it in the clothes closet. (He often tells this incident to interviewers.) But the most important part of the novel is the ending, when on the day of his 50th birthday Chinaski/Bukowski hands in his resignation. He leaves the post office. He has decided to become a full-time writer.

Bukowski doesn't mind repeating himself in his stories. For example, you'll find in *Notes of a Dirty Old Man* the original of an episode that is told detail for detail in *Post Office*—the one about the nymphomaniac wife who topples a vase of geraniums on her husband's back while they are making love, who tells Chinaski about her lovers and the "guy with the purple stick pin," and who disgusts Chinaski because he eats snails. Yet readers who compare versions will see marked progress from the stories as they appeared in underground publications, contrasted to the way the same material is used in his later books. Bukowski's style, which has always been assured, grows more fluent, more seemingly spontaneous, and more filled with the self-irony that falls short of the cynicism marking his later books. He has found the key to mixing intense personal feeling with denunciation of social conditions—a kind of anarchic individualism.

The portrait of Betty, who dies alone in the hospital from total negligence of doctors and nurses, will ring more than one bell with everyone who was ever unfortunate enough to have a relative hospitalized. Such dramatic visions of the world are typical of Bukowski, and crop up many times. An example is the story of two parrots who see their two keepers in mourning and squawk: "What do those two know about grief, always closed in their little cage?" Or again with Betty, when Chinaski sees her after their divorce: "She went back to her room and put on her best dress, high heels, tried to fix up, but there was a terrible sadness about her . . . It was sad, it was sad, it was sad . . . we had both been robbed."

The general tone of *Post Office* epitomizes Bukowski's entire output—a mixture of desolation and humor, imbuing every scene. His house furnishings are always wretched: "I opened my door. There was nobody in there. The furniture was old and ripped, the rug almost colorless. Empty beer cans on the floor. I was in the right place." Or when Chinaski/Bukowski mistakenly enters the apartment of another tenant—living quarters nice and clean in distinct contrast to his own. Then he goes to his own apartment, where he lives with the mother of his daughter:

"There was nothing in the refrigerator. I walked to the sink. It was stopped up with garbage. The dirty dishes filled half the sink and on top of the water along with a few paper plates, floated these jars and jar lids." But the scene becomes true Bukowski with his comment to the woman: "I know you want to save the world. But can't you start with the kitchen?"

He can direct the same kind of humor at himself, as when he is portrays himself as a Humphrey Bogart type of character: "I slapped her . . . I slapped her again . . . I grabbed that blue dress by the neck and ripped one side of it down to her waist." Or "I swung and he walked right into it. I got him in the mouth. His whole mouth was broken teeth and blood. Hector dropped to his knees, crying, holding his mouth with both hands . . . Then as Hector was crying I walked up and booted him in the ass. He sprawled flat on the floor, still crying. I walked over, took a pull at his beer." Or, as when he is talking to the mulatto who persecuted him and says, "It was Chambers looking at me . . . I walked over to a trashcan, and still looking at him, I spit. Then I walked off. Chambers never bothered me again."

In 1972, the year after *Post Office* came out, Ferlinghetti's City Lights published *Erections, Ejaculations, Exhibitions and General Tales of Ordinary Madness*. The book multiplied his fame in the literary world of America and Europe. The American edition noted that after 18 or 20 books of poetry and prose, and after having been published in *Story* and *Portfolio III*, Bukowski had stopped writing for ten years. It was a ten year period of drinking, at the end of which he found himself at the general hospital in Los Angeles and almost died. It was following this that he went to work at the post office and began writing a column for *Open City*. He left his postal job, he says, "to avoid going crazy." It is now impossible for him to work for others, he declares, and the way his typewriter eats up ribbons shows how completely he has turned to working for himself.

Bukowski's world never changes: he is always the main character seen with pitying compassion or ferocious disdain, but always with a powerful self-irony. Inevitably there are plenty of more or less pretty women around, all possessed of unlimited sexual appetite and a marked predeliction for drinking.

South of No North

    South of No North, a collection of 27 stories, appeared in 1973, published by John Martin's Black Sparrow Press. While Bukowski sometimes appears as the usual Henry Chinaski, named Hank, or as Carl (a writer that feels he has reached the end), or as Randall Harris, the stories do not change. The places and the themes are Bukowski's world of sex, alcohol, horse racings and boxing. The style is like Hemingway, and the dialogues show a wise ability and a lot of cunning.

    Several stories describe the writer as he is doing his readings in different cities, with his travels and his adventures during his journeys and his many drunken episodes, naturally, but the majority of the stories describe the enervating hard and humble jobs that tormented the writer for years before he got settled in the post office.

    One story not true to form is "Politics," where he describes his astonishing position as a Nazi during college years. It is a position that often leaves interviewers dumfounded. However, the Naziism of Bukowski has a very special twist. It is based on rebellion to conformity; and it melts like snow under the sun when a real live Nazi commits acts of violence.

Bukowski says:

"At L.A. City College just before World War II, I posed as a Nazi. I hardly knew Hitler from Hercules and cared less. It was just that sitting in class and hearing all the 'patriots' preach how we should go over and do the beast in. I grew bored. I decided to become the opposition . . . However, I really didn't have any political beliefs. It was a way of floating free. I played Nazi for some time longer, while caring neither for the Nazis nor the Communists nor the Americans . . . I didn't feel much like going to war and I didn't feel much like being a conscientious objector either."

He tells how a real Nazi threw rotten tomatoes at a Communist who was making a speech from a podium.

"I lost control of my disciples that day and walked away as they started hurling the tomatoes."

Several Bukowski stories from *South of No North* describe the writer as he goes from city to city, doing readings—his travels and adventures and, as you would expect, his many drunken episodes. But the majority of the stories describe the hard, humble, enervating jobs that tormented him for years, before he finally signed on with the post office.

There is also the story "Remember Pearl Harbor" about his arrest for dodging the draft and being given a psychiatric exam. He talks willingly:

Psychiatrist: "Do you believe in war?"

Bukowski: "No."

Psychiatrist: "Are you willing to go to war?"

Bukowski: "Yes."

Psychiatrist: "I want you to come to my party. Will you come?"

Bukowski: "No."

Bukowski explains to us:

"I almost wanted the war. Yet, at the same time, I was glad to be out of it . . . My objection to war was not that I had to kill somebody or be killed senselessly, that hardly mattered."

Too bad for those who try to find a political ideology in Bukowski. He was anarchical through and through and was a rebel as no one else could be.

His ideal of the male is revealed in the story, "Guts." Bukowski tells us:

"I have always admired the villain, the outlaw, the son-of-a-bitch. I don't like the clean-shaven boy with the necktie and the good job. I like desperate men, men with broken teeth and broken minds and broken ways . . . I'm more interested in perverts than saints. I can relax with bums because I am a bum. I don't like laws, morals, religions, rules. I don't like to be shaped by society."

It was a society Bukowski had known only in its cruelest aspect, that of poverty. In *Confessions of a Man Insane Enough to Live with Beasts*, his account of the general hospital to which he was taken as a teenager tells how they opened his pimples with an electric drill; and later, when he was an adult, how he was taken there close to death, hemorrhaging due to alcoholism, and they left him passed out on the floor.

In the same story, and with the same tone, Bukowski tells us his experiences in a slaughterhouse; and a marriage that is arranged by mail with the publisher of a literary magazine in Texas who, it later turns out, is a nymphomaniac and a multi-millionaire. I could go on talking about the evergrowing drama and the extraordinary fluency of his writing, which has now been purged of rhetoric, melodramatic exaggeration, and indulgence in vernacular excess. But I would rather underline the presence of landscape description—very rare in

Bukowski—that at most talked about "pale rays of sun between the dirty venetian blinds."

The landscape he introduces in "A Couple of Winos" is a landscape of complete squalor and desperation: "I was walking up the road, it was dusty and dirty and hot . . . I looked around; there was only sand and cliffs and the oven dry bright yellow sun and no place to go." This is the landscape fixed in Bukowski. He never mentions the flowers, the roses, the fruit trees that surround his home in San Pedro.

Factotum

No less squalid is the urban landscape of his Los Angeles in his second novel, *Factotum*, all very short chapters, shorter than a story and longer than a sketch tell about the adventures of a young Bukowski, pre-post office. It came out in 1975, one year after publication of his poetry collection, *Burning in Water, Drowning in Flame*. In chapter 86 he writes, "I had walked back down the street alone noticing for the first time the pieces of blown paper and accumulated trash that littered the street."

More and more identifying with his anti-hero figure, Henry Chinaski, Bukowski writes from the log of his travels from New Orleans to Los Angeles to New York to Philadelphia to St. Louis to Miami and then back to Los Angeles again, travels punctuated by menial jobs kept only a few days or a few weeks. Bukowski describes how weighed down and humiliated he felt because of them. It reminds one of the proletariat novels of the naturalistic 1930s, but Bukowski escapes the overly dramatic tone of the writers who denounced such working conditions without knowing them first hand.

Bukowski knows them first hand, having experienced them for years. He knows the futility, falsity, and comic side of them. He also knows the struggle it takes to achieve a few

130

hours of open air or a few moments of mirth. He knows the torment of getting caught in an occupation he doesn't believe in, without compatible companions to share thoughts and hopes. Hope is always in the background even though it is a story of desperation. The desperation is bone-deep. Only hope sustains Bukowski. "That is all a man needed: hope. I was lack of hope that discourages a man."

Dog biscuit factory, women's clothing firm, bicycle and spare parts yard, neon light installation company, brake factory—the hope of finding something better is slight, but it glimmers on. Bukowski worked as a store keeper, cab driver, ambulance driver, tomato picker, and janitor at a newspaper plant, all the while going from one drunken spree to another. He went from one hooker to another, too: Laura, Jan, Mary Lou—the list is so lengthy it is impossible to name them all.

At long last something changed: a magazine accepts one of his stories. The letter he receives says:

"We are returning these four stories but we are keeping one. We have been watching your work for a long time and we are most happy to accept this story."

Bukowski says:

"I got up from the chair still holding my acceptance slip. My first. From the number one literary magazine in America. Never had the world looked so good, so full of promise. I walked over to the bed, sat down, read it again. I studied each curve in the handwriting of Gladmore's signature. I got up, walked the acceptance slip over to the dresser, propped it there. Then I undressed, turned out the lights and went to bed. I couldn't sleep. I got up, turned on the light, walked over to the dresser and read it again."

This moving confession captures all the hopes and anxieties of the frustrated writer and is a reverse image of the hope-starved confessions of his vagabond life. Wrapped up in it is an exoneration of sorts of the conflict with his parents. He remembers them as heartless. They took him in between travels, but kept track of each and every expense thus incurred, on the condition he would pay them back as soon as he found a job. "You don't have any ambition," his father told him. "You don't have any get-up-and-go. How the hell are you going to make it in this world?" The father bailed him out of jail for being drunk—a 30 dollar sum—and made clear his humiliation at having such a son, telling Bukowski "It's bad enough you don't want to serve your country in time of war."

Humiliation, discouragement, total lack of communication—these are the things Bukowski thinks of when he speaks of his parents. He writes of the father trying to force the son's face into his own drunken vomit and of the son socking him in defense. This episode occurs in chapter 11 of the book, and Bukowski repeats it often in interviews.

Other episodes are recycled, like the one in chapter 7 where migrant workers are given cans of food without can openers so the food can be used again. Or as the one in chapter 17 where the main character is sold a suit that destroys itself even while he is wearing it. Or the ones in chapters 32, 33, 34, and 35 where the multimillionaire without an arm throws coins on the floor when he is drunk, is always surrounded by hookers, asks Chinaski to write a plot for the opera he has composed, and takes everyone on his boat.

Repeated episodes do not mean identical episodes. The stories are the same, but different. It is as if they cannot be eradicated from Bukowski's mind; as if he is haunted by the memory of events lived without joy and without involvement. So he tells them again and again.

"Frankly, I was horrified by life, at what a man had to do simply in order to eat, sleep, and keep himself clothed. So I stayed in bed and drank. When you drank the world was still out there, but for the moment it didn't have you by the throat."

His desperation is always wrapped in self-irony and humor—for example, when Chinaski says: "I'm a genius, but nobody knows it outside of me." Or when he says: "Did anyone ever tell you how funny you are? (No.) It doesn't surprise me." Other examples of his self-irony and humor can be found in his dialogue with bosses at work, with hookers, with companions at the bar, throughout the aimless odyssey of the man who has no ambition, finds only hard and humble jobs to live from, is indifferent to society's ideals, and has no traditional decency.

He doesn't fight against the futility of the universe, he simply points out the absolute lack of meaning in a life alienated by depersonalization, enslaved by economic needs, and paralyzed by the impossibility of breaking free from the short path that leads to the grave.

Themes in Bukowski are not much different than those chosen by certain other American writers of the rebellious 1950s and '60s, so in a sense he is on the fringe of the proletarian or subproletarian school of writing. But there is a difference. Bukowski aspires to be a poet.

His style in his later work is far removed from the ingenuousness of his beginning. As a mature writer his voice is that of an experienced story-teller with a sober style, direct yet evocative, reminiscent of Hemingway. Even more strongly derivative is his humor, which he traces to one of his idols, John Fante. Bukowski never tires of acknowledging his debt to Fante's style. He thought so much of Fante that he prevailed upon John Martin of Black Sparrow Press to have Fante's out-of-print books reissued.

In *Factotum*, Bukowski draws the picture of a man who faces modern urban life and finds it grotesque and meaningless. The man's desperation and despair, his squalid and hopeless state, all resound vividly thanks to Bukowski's indisputable skillfulness in the telling. The man is too horrified to be a cynic. He feels he is inside a kind of huge ridiculous theatre.

Love is a Dog From Hell

In 1977, his fourth important collection of poems was published: *Love is a Dog from Hell.* It joined the others previously published: *The Days Run Away Like Wild Horses Over the Hills* (1969), *Mockingbird Wish Me Luck* (1972), and *Burning in Water, Drowning in Flame,* (selected poems 1955-1973 with a foreword by the author, 1974.) This new collection put the final touch on his image as a tough poet: direct, rough, unmusical, firm in refusing the least concession to classic tradition; a poet who writes on unpoetic subjects; who seems unacquainted with metric rules; and who gives no quarter to the kind of romanticism that permeates popular American literature, where drunks are noble, hookers are sensitive, and artists unlucky.

Pessimism alternates with self-pity; in other words, what unfolds is the catalogue of Bukowski's life. He has based his stories and poems on it. Yet he knows he writes in a way that can reach everyone. Grief, humor, and violence are qualities everyone can understand. His alcoholism, too. The whole spectrum of death and solitude is powerfully expressed.

Someone said these poems are about people who live in a death world. For example, in one poem he describes a school ceremony his daughter attended when she was six years old. He compares the blooming innocence of the children with the grey gravelike decay of the parents there.

There is an almost random note to the places he finds his characters; yet they are always the lowest of the low.

Jim Metro of the *Montgomery* (Alabama) *Advertiser Journal* of September 7, 1975 stated that, murder and robbery aside, Bukowski could be compared to Francois Villon, and that both of them may be considered forerunners of Mickey Spillane. Rash comments? Perhaps. But they show how one critic in the American outland views Bukowski, for Bukowski has reached beyond the big cities and become a voice heard everywhere.

Bukowski never wearies of presenting again and again his world of misery, desperation, poverty, nightmares about old age, fury, impatience for everything and everybody, predeliction for lawless types, knife always ready in his pocket, his paean to a life based on morning and evening hangovers, and the sexual intercourse that is often frustrated by having too much to drink. This is the substance of a crude and messy poetry that vibrates with the experiences cited. It is not even a poetry of protest or denunciation. It is not of the "Beat Generation." It is sometimes only amusing, satirical, or dramatic. But even though its style may be purposely used to bait imitators, it is wholly original and defies comparison to Jeffers, Pound, and Ginsberg.

Bukowski has said that writing a poem is like writing a letter—a definition if we really need one. Perhaps it is the very personal images he is thinking of, the extraordinarily evocative power of them. He has the skillfulness to build horrifying portraits that form the mini-stories of the modern human condition. His key, we know, is his life, a certain kind of life, a life of horror and disgust.

The poems sing the streets, the hippie life, the bars, fast food, cockroach-infested furnished rooms, and everything that is mired in the blood and dirt of an unfocused existence. The people who read them include parking attendants, jailed prisoners, hospital patients, and the disenfranchised everywhere who write letters of admiration and ask for copies of his books. (In his interview Bukowski says with satisfaction that he prefers these requests to the ones from students who can afford to buy them.)

Ben Pleasants, in the *Los Angeles Times* has written: "Perhaps Bukowski is the best poet of his generation; but the critics, women's lib, Marxists, and reviewers of the main newspapers and magazines prefer to ignore him. In the meantime he is written about in *Le Monde*, the *Times Literary Supplement, Spiegel, Stern,* and in countless other European magazines."

I don't know if Bukowski is "the best poet of his generation," but unquestionably he is read with a sense of connection if not passion, by those attuned to real life, or, if you want, by the man in the street.

Women

In *Women* as in *Factotum* he once more trots out the immature black sheep, irresponsible, immoral, broke, without a job, alcoholic, impotent—autobiographical stuff, of course; only here it is centered around some 20 experiences he's had with females after four years of abstinence.

When Bukowski wrote *Women* he was already well-known, more in Europe than in America as many reviews of his earlier *Factotum* had shown. In *Women,* did the memory of his past suffering make it seem misanthropic? Or his love of classical music and refined culture make it seem more intellectual? Possibly. In *Women,* too, Bukowski hides under invented names for some of the real characters of his life. Douglas Blazek, who had published *A Bukowski Sampler* in 1969 becomes Doug Patrick. The sweet Linda Lee Beighle, who has lived with him for several years now, becomes Sara. The poetess Linda King, with whom he had a stormy three-year relationship, becomes Lydia Vance. And "Cupcakes" O'Brien, who in 1976 inspired him to write the poetry collection, *Scarlet*, becomes Tammie.

Bukowski writes the book without uncertainties now (if he ever had them). There is an unmistakable fluency and ease—clearly the result of long experience.

Bukowski is conscious of being among the important writers. "You're Chinaski, Chinaski the legend," he says of himself. "You've got an image." He sleeps in the dorm at the university after a reading, but he does not hesitate to openly express his scorn for all official culture.

Responding to the goads of interviewers and the curiosity of the mass media, Bukowski tries to explain his technique of writing:

"I just exist. Then later I try to remember, and write some of it down."

Or he harks back to the hard times:

"I remembered the old days, living on one candy bar a day, sending out hand printed stories to *The Atlantic Monthly* and *Harper's*."

Or, when asked if drinking has impaired his writing:

"No. I'm just an alcoholic who became a writer so I could stay in bed until noon."

Humor was his out. Some things, he felt, were so obvious he could make a joke of them. But it would be a mistake to think his use of humor diluted his basic sense of desperation and fury. It did not.

Near the beginning of *Women* Bukowski writes such lines as "I have a great dislike, both for freeways and for instructions." Or "Humanity—you never had it from the beginning. That was my motto." He tries a psychoanalytic interpretation of his animosity: "It was my childhood, you see. I never knew what love was." He repeats these very words later on: "It was my childhood, you see. No love, no affection."

137

Immediately, self-pity turns into self-irony. He describes himself as a hunted animal. A woman says of him: "Your face seems kind. But your eyes—they're beautiful. They're wild, crazy, like some animal peering out of a forest on fire. God, something like that."

Then he gives us a pitiless self-portrait:

"And there I was, 225 pounds, perpetually lost and confused, short legs, ape-like upper body, all chest, no neck, head too large, blurred eyes, hair uncombed, six feet of geek."

He ends by identifying himself with the specter of death:

"I was a conquering army, I was a rapist, I was her master, I was death."

Death is always present in this book. A sentence in chapter 26 is very revealing:

"I was old and I was ugly . . . Was I trying to screw my way past death? By being with young girls did I hope I wouldn't grow old, feel old? I just didn't want to age badly, simply quit, be dead before death itself arrived."

A similar frame of reference returns when he says:

"The dead were fucking the dead" or "Just living until you die is hard work."

But in the last page of the book his relationship with Sara/Linda offers a sop to the critics and a gleam of hope:

"Sara was a good woman. I had to get myself straightened out . . . A man could lose his identity fucking around too much. Sara deserved much better."

By these lights you can re-evaluate Bukowski. Behind his denunciations is the most catholic of Puritans: "The thought of sex as something forbidden excited me beyond all reason." And: "There is a lot of puritan in me. Puritans might enjoy sex more than anybody."

But in spite of this, the book's background is still squalor, still horror. When he is promised an "unimaginable feeling" if he will take the preferred mescaline he replies: "I've felt that without any help at all."

What about women? What does Bukowski think about women? In chapter 94, he reveals his thoughts. The chapter's title is even in italics.

"*Women*: I liked the colors of their clothing . . . the cruelty in some faces . . . they had it over us: they planned much better and were better organized. While men were watching professional football or drinking beer or bowling, they, the women—were thinking about us, concentrating, studying, deciding whether to accept us, discard us, exchange us, kill us, or whether simply to leave us . . . No matter what they did, we ended up lonely and insane."

So much for the "tough guy," the macho image. This Don Quixote of the double beds, this Casanova without little golden balls to stick into the vagina, wilts into a laughing-stock in the presence of powers bigger than he. He's sincere when he says he doesn't understand the fury the feminists feel against him. He says that in reality it is not him who treats women as objects, but women who treat him that way—a view that shows up both in his books and real life. In this novel, called by an American critic "superb," women are always portrayed with irreverence but also with a perception that describes the personality as well as the body. Other authors may lapse into sentimentality at such times, but not Bukowski. He looks at them with the same cold, lucid detachment he brings to playing the horses. His insensitivity toward his sex-partner takes second place to his self-irony, however. In sexual intercourse, Bukowski finds pity and sympathy as only a man of experience could conceive.

"I had to taste women in order to really know them ... I could invent men because I was one, but women, for me, were almost impossible to fictionalize without first knowing them. So I explored them as best I could and found human beings inside."

Then when the affair went wrong he'd feel what it was like to be truly lonely and crazed, and thus know what he must face, finally, when his own end came.

Bukowski's old uncle Heinrich lived in Germany. He was in his 90s, and Bukowski and Linda Lee went to visit him. The trip didn't last long; about two weeks. They made a quick stop in Mannheim, where Carl Weissner lives. Weissner was the one who translated Bukowski's books into German, as he also translated William Burroughs, Allen Ginsberg, and Bob Dylan. Bukowski owed him a great deal for his success in Europe. They visited a few castles—Schwetzingen, Heidelberg—before doing a reading in Hamburg. The auditorium had only 800 seats, but 1,200 people managed to get in, leaving 300 outside.

After Hamburg, they went to Andernach, his birth town, where his uncle lives, and found the home where Bukowski was born. It was up for sale after having been a whorehouse for a long time. Bukowski didn't miss the chance to go to Dusseldorf to see the horse races; nor to Cologne, where they underwent the typical adventure of lost tickets, wrong trains, and a visit to two friends in the middle of the night. They went to Nice to visit Linda's mother, Serena; and Bukowski was a guest on an ill-fated TV show in Paris.

Shakespeare Never Did This

Telling of all this travel would be meaningless except for two things: one, it was the only European journey Bukowski made; and two, it inspired this writer to pen one of his best books—*Shakespeare Never Did This*—an honest autobiography without sexual and alcoholic exaggerations. It is imbued with the sense of melancholy, desperation, and fear which, without doubt, are the hallmarks of his poetic world. It was published in 1979 by City Lights, with many photos by Michael Monfort. In 25 chapters it gives a step by step account of their time in Europe.

The book tells of the scandal that erupted on French TV when Bukowski was asked to leave—or, more precisely, was thrown out as a rowdy drunk. Unfortunately, he doesn't comment on the demonstration against him organized by German women's lib. But the pages are full of notes about death as he made us familiar with it in *Women*. He observed guys at the bar who "were waiting to die but they were in no particular hurry." He thought about many things:

"If a woman wants to sell her parts it's probably not much different than a concert violinist up there doing his concerto—It's survival anyway you know how, death will be along but better to trick it into waiting a while." The image of death is always linked to those of terror, grief, and horror

He writes: "(The cathedral) almost made me wish I could accept the Christian God instead of my tiny 17 gods of protection because one big God would have helped me understand some of the whores I had lived with and of the women, the dull jobs, the no jobs, the nights of madness and starvation . . ."

And: "I was not a thinking man, I went by what I felt and my feelings went to the crippled, the tortured, the damned and the lost, not out of sympathy but out of brotherhood because I was one of them, lost, confused, indecent, petty, fearful and cowardly."

Also: "The Big God just had too many guns for me. He was too right and too powerful. I didn't want to be forgiven or accepted or found, I wanted something less than death, something not too much. Death meant little to me. I was the last joke in a series of bad jokes."

And: "Death was another movie."

And: "Death only caused problems to those left behind who had some relationship with the deceased."

And: "Some people enter the world with wealth but they all leave broke."

In case you had any doubts, Bukowski has never been at peace within himself.

Almost at the end of the book he says: "Well, I'd finish my 3rd novel and 3 good novels was all a man could ask for. Of course I was thinking about the 4th—about my childhood, but childhood novels were almost impossible . . . And I was afraid of it."

6

STAGE AND SCREEN

Rising as they do from his violent and corrupted life, Bukowski's stories have inspired the director Marco Ferreri to make a movie from some of them. The movie is entitled *Tales of Ordinary Madness.* Out of the 64 stories contained in *Erections, Ejaculations, Exhibitions and General Tales of Ordinary Madness,* four in particular prompted the motion picture, Ferreri said, yet there are mainly two you'll recognize: "The Most Beautiful Girl in Town" and "Rape! Rape!"

In 1981 Ferreri brought his movie to the Venice Film Festival for screening. He had shot it in the United States and in the process spent a few hours with Bukowski in a motel on Sunset Boulevard, where the film's staff was staying. They talked for a couple of hours as the tape recorder ran. The slow deliberate cadences of Bukowski's speech strike a familiar chord because they are the very ones he uses with all interviewers, probably (as he thinks) in the interest of clear understanding. Several audio tape cassettes were used up in the process.

"I never drink," said Ferreri, "but with him I got drunk. We didn't talk much; we kissed and tried to see who could outdrink the other."

With Ferreri's comments becoming happier as the minutes go by, the joint laughter, the faux pas of the translators, and the speeches becoming slurry at the end, thanks to the wine, the tapes make interesting listening.

Bukowski:

"I don't like people. I haven't changed my mind. They are living shits."

"You see me as a crab trapped in a net, but in reality I am the net."

"Oh shit, we sit here looking at each other. What are we trying to do . . . or prove?"

"I've got to win, always, or I become unhappy."

"When I wake up from a nightmare I'm 79."

"The more you drink, the better you live."

"You're a good man, but you need help."

"If I don't succeed in doing what I want to, I don't care about anything else. I have to type every night, go to the races every day, be clean with no crap."

"You are a tough guy, but you're getting drunk. I drink a lot, but I don't have to prove it. Why do you want to?"

"I only write when I'm drunk, but I don't know what I write."

"You've got to stop drinking. It's bad for your health, it's bad for your kidneys."

"Drinking doesn't hurt my brain. On the contrary."

Ferreri answers logically at the start of the performance, but eventually the wine takes hold.

Ferreri on the tape:

"No, I don't have to prove anything."

"I drink because you drink."

"Come on, for two bottles of wine you don't have to be so hard."

"You write your poems and don't worry."

144

"You do it your way and I do it my way. Anyway, starting from this evening I love you much."

"You write beautiful words, beautiful images, images more beautiful than words."

That was Ferreri on the tape. He now says to us: "Five or six years ago I fell in love with Bukowski's books, rather than with Bukowski. That's the key to my movie. I was interested in the places, in the images; and I found in the States the very images he had caused me to imagine. Bukowski is a very visual author. What appealed to me were those images, those characters, those streets and homes where they lived, the Los Angeles he writes about.

"I had at the back of my mind, an American stage design; I wanted to make my film echo this. I chose Bukowski because of his images of course, but also for his words. When our world is crumbling, the phenomenon of vulgarity comes back; people want to hear bad words. For such a time as ours I wanted to choose a language that is not ordinary in the classic sense, but vulgar-poetic, as in Bukowski.

"It's hard to live in the States as Bukowski did. The images found in his writing are word-pictures of the ghettos, of repression, of oppression; and dialogue that becomes poetry, the spirit of his rebellion expressed with vulgarity of language. If today we feel the need to make a movie based on American images it is because we are on the outskirts of an empire that gives us only official images—images we must resist."

Everybody knows everything about Ferreri's movie: He wrote the screenplay with Sergio Amidei. He did the editing with Ruggero Mastroianni, Marcello's brother. He has chosen such actors as Ben Gazzara, Ornella Muti, and Susanne Tyrrel—people who have played in Bukowski adaptations onstage. Ferreri's observations about Bukowski are very intense, even as his film adaptation is very sharp. But the thousands of people who have seen the movie know this.

Another director, Patrick Ross, made a TV movie from *South of No North*, a volume of 27 tales subtitled "Stories of the Buried Life" (published by Black Sparrow Press in 1973.) Ross is a young man born and raised in Germany. The movie is 40 minutes long, was shot in Los Angeles in 16mm, cost $60,000, and features Jack Kehoe and Raymond Mayo as the two robbers of the story, with Ann Ramsey and Susanne Tyrrel playing the two female characters. In a parody of Hitchcock movies where the director played a role himself, Bukowski appears onscreen sitting in a train, reciting a brief monologue that ends concisely with one of the maxims that recur in some of his books:

"It seems that a man has only two choices: do something or become a vagabond."

The movie was shown for the first time in 1981 at the Gordon Theatre in Hollywood. Bukowski attended. The young director hoped to sell the movie to American or European TV, and to adapt seven more stories from the same collection for the TV screen. Bukowski has encouraged him to do it, even though in his many interviews he repeats:

"I never go to the movies. I hate it."

An Italian theatre group, La Cooperative Gran Serraglio, has also been inspired by Bukowski stories. The group has done a biographical play prompted by five stories from *South of No North* and the dialogue between Bobby and Hank taken from *Notes of a Dirty Old Man*. The writer was played onstage by Richy Ferrero and the director was Mariano Meli. For the occasion Silvia Bizio, who teaches in Los Angeles, taped a 45-minute interview on video. (If I'm not mistaken, this has been sold to Italian TV.)

When you point out to Ferrero that he has missed the swollen beer belly of Bukowski, he answers that his portrayal

146

reflects the young Bukowski. When you point out to the director that the desolate room of the stage set is very different from the clean California home where Bukowski now lives, he answers that the set represents the place Bukowski lived 30 years ago in East Los Angeles, a bad area.

Director Meli says that with their mix of alcohol, sex, and violence, Bukowski's books are linked together by an endless desperation, themes that are the moving forces of the play. The script follows Bukowski's text with rigorous fidelity. Thus, the main character can break loose to Bukowski's "high-fantasy world, haunted by sadness and sorrows even more realistic than the vomit and recurrent copulations" of the stories themselves.

Performer Ferrero says: "If you can succeed in portraying his sanguine values and at the same time his bestial strengths, you can capture both sides of the man, Bukowski."

The movie and theatrical adaptations, the 64 stories, the pieces already published in the underground press and literary magazines of the establishment, remind us in a certain way how the stylistic attempts in *Notes of a Dirty Old Man* simply foreshadowed the structures Bukowski would use in his future novels.

Marco Ferreri, Ben Gazzara and Bukowski meet to discuss the film *Tales of Ordinary Madness*, based on Bukowski's short stories (1980).

Photo: Joe Wolberg

7
SUMMING UP

Between sheets wet with sperm, empty beer cans, stinky sweat under the armpits, cockroaches all over the walls, Bukowski wanders around his zone of decadence, sex, violence, and alcoholism, and his dreams crumble.

They are illusions, lies of our time, resonating with deliberate indecency, true stories in the huge indifference of space. In his fear and loneliness he finds again his humanity, self-being, sense of the ridiculous, irreverent sympathy, and expresses it with the detachment of a horse player.

Readers, especially the critics, sometimes notice only the sensational or "obscene" aspects. But Bukowski, under his mask—or what he calls "being a clown"—continues to reveal his disconcerting intimacy with the deformities of life. One strength of his story-telling often lies in his use of the first person voice—the autobiographical mode.

He sees alcohol as self-defense by the frightened individual against an absurd and terrifying destiny. It is never glorified as a virtue or salvation. At most, it is seen as an escape: "You have to find something while you are waiting to die. It's great to have the possibility of a choice."

His fears, his maxims, his confessions, come to the surface in a style that seems spontaneous, but in reality must be credited to years of severe discipline in composing poems and stories. It is a style that gives unity to everything he writes. Out of his own experiences, it features a nihilism that is hopeless, without a single ray of light: women are all hookers, friendships last as long as a beer, books are not understood by critics, society is collapsing, flaws and corruption triumph in this world, our destiny is only death and defeat.

So what is in Bukowski's books that appeals to a steadily increasing audience of readers? What hypnotizes people to read his increasingly desperate pages?

The easiest answer is simply his candor.

During one interview Bukowski said: "Why can't a poet tell us directly what he has to say? Why must it be interpreted? This is not a little game for beginners who exchange cute words. Nobody ever came out of a reading saying 'Jesus, I feel like I'm dying.' Nobody, do you understand?"

There is no doubt that Bukowski continues to write that he feels as if he's dying. But that is not all he writes. With the same simplicity and frankness he confronts the everyday insanities that, cumulatively, can lead to the mental hospital. His denunciation of these small disasters is nothing less than, in the long run, a denunciation of the social system.

Europeans may respond more readily than Americans to Bukowski's expressionist style, with its abysses of desperation and disgust, but his pages contain a portrait of the United States that is often overlooked by Europeans whose only view of the U.S.A. is of a dream continent. Not even the pressures of anti-capitalist political ideology have succeeded in breaking the myths promulgated by U.S. movies and records. Ironically, not in the slums of the poor, which Bukowski knew so well as a young man, but in the middle-class lap of well-being is where Bukowski now has him home, with a bank account in very high sums.

If you ask Bukowski to name his favorite writer, the one who influenced him most, he will answer: John Fante. Fante is a neorealistic writer of the 1930s, a man of Italian ancestry, born in Denver, Colorado, in 1911, who now lives in Los Angeles. He suffers from diabetes and is confined to a wheelchair. In 1938 he published *Wait Until Spring, Bandini*; in 1939 *Ask the Dust*; in 1940 *Dago Red*; and in 1952 *Full of Life*. But if you ask Bukowski who he would like to become, he answers "Hemingway" and says it with the same humility with which Norman Mailer once answered the same question with the same answer. Clearly, Bukowski's writing is closer to Hemingway than to Henry Miller or Jack Kerouac, in spite of pronouncements of the popular press—yet it is totally his own. If resemblances are needed (are they?) it might be said his drinking had more in common with Hemingway's Lost Generation than with the Beat Generation of Kerouac.

Jack Kerouac has little in common with Bukowski. Kerouac's splendid prose is regarded as the most brilliant of this American half-century. His plots tell of the dramatic swing between alcohol's destructiveness and its seeming input of explosive vital energy. This blends with an awed overwhelming enthusiasm for the beauty of the world and of life. Kerouac has much in common with Zen doctrine, where life is an illusion, a mere waiting room to the void of Buddhism.

All this is absent in Bukowski. The only place where they meet is the drinking, but Bukowski talks of alcohol as the writers of the 1920s did, as a midway on which to be happy, and a trick to escape reality. He talks of it as a cursed writer, which may account for some of his appeal to Europeans. As for Henry Miller, their work meets at only one point: the descriptions of sexual intercourse. Love for the human body that in Miller ranges widely, from the triumph of sex to the tragedy of illness, in Bukowski does not exist—not even when both writers are observing the natural world.

In reality, I would put aside such comparisons, be they positive or negative. I would like to give a compliment to Bukowski and consider him an absolute original. He is outside even the "cursed" writers like Celine and Artaud.

To define Bukowski's way as a writer—creating through the images of everyday life distorted under a colossal enlarging lens—is to define Bukowski's way of living. Both are anarchic and crazy, violent and brutal, always sarcastic, cruel and very bitter, purged of sentimentality, soaked with distaste and distrust of human kind, and for society as a whole. Perhaps that is what appeals to young Europeans facing cultural crises, and certainly to the punk rebellion for his proposed negation of all indulgences and strict daily habits. We could compare Bukowski's totally negative interpretation of life to that of the punks, but that would place Bukowski in a decadent dimension, which I would not like to do.

I would rather like to think of a perverse and romantic Bukowski, vital in his disgust, creative in his horrified drama, and tragic in his loss of hope in any direction whatsoever; a Bukowski sunk in the catastrophe; which is the catastrophe of the chaos we are living.

BOOKS BY CHARLES BUKOWSKI

Flower, Fist and Bestial Wail (1960)

Longshot Pomes for Broke Players (1962)

Run with the Hunted (1962)

It Catches My Heart in Its Hands (1963)

Crucifix in a Deathhand (1965)

Cold Dogs in the Courtyard (1965)

Confessions of a Man Insane Enough to Live with Beasts (1965)

All the Assholes in the World and Mine (1966)

At Terror Street and Agony Way (1968)

Poems Written Before Jumping out of an 8 Story Window (1968)

Notes of a Dirty Old Man (1969)

The Days Run Away Like Wild Horses Over the Hills (1969)

Fire Station (1970)

Post Office (1971)

Mockingbird Wish Me Luck (1972)

Erections, Ejaculations, Exhibitions and General Tales of Ordinary Madness
          (1972)

South of No North (1973)

Burning in Water, Drowning in Flame: Selected Poems 1955-1973 (1974)

Factotum (1975)

Love is a Dog from Hell: Poems 1974-1977 (1977)

Women (1978)

Play the Piano Drunk/Like a Percussion Instrument/Until the Fingers Begin to
          Bleed a Bit (1979)

Dangling in the Tournefortia (1981)

Ham on Rye (1982)

Bring Me Your Love (1983)

Hot Water Music (1983)

There's No Business (1984)

War All the Time: Poems 1981-1984 (1984)

You Get So Alone at Times That It Just Makes Sense (1986)

The Movie: "Barfly" (1987)

The Roominghouse Madrigals: Early Selected Poems 1946-1966 (1988)

Hollywood (1989)

Septuagenarian Stew: Stories & Poems (1990)

The Last Night of the Earth Poems (1992)

Run with the Hunted: A Charles Bukowski Reader (1993)

Screams from the Balcony: Selected Letters 1960-1970, Volume I (1993)

Pulp (1994)

Shakespeare Never Did This (augmented edition) (1995)

Living on Luck: Selected Letters 1960s-1970s, Volume 2 (1995)

Betting on the Muse: Poems & Stories (1996)

Bone Palace Ballet: New Poems (1997)

The Captain Is Out to Lunch and the Sailors Have Taken over the Ship (1998)

Reach for the Sun: Selected Letters 1978-1994, Volume 3 (1999)

What Matters Most is How Well You Walk Through the Fire (1999)

NAME INDEX

BOOKS BY SUN DOG PRESS

STEVE RICHMOND, *Santa Monica Poems*

STEVE RICHMOND, *Hitler Painted Roses* (Foreword by Charles Bukowski)

STEVE RICHMOND, *Spinning Off Bukowski*

NEELI CHERKOVSKI, *Elegy for Bob Kaufman*

RANDALL GARRISON, *Lust in America*

BILLY CHILDISH, *Notebooks of a Naked Youth*

DAN FANTE, *Chump Change*

ROBERT STEVEN RHINE, *My Brain Escapes Me*

HOWARD BONE, with DANIEL WALDRON, *Side Show: My Life with Geeks, Freaks, & Vagabonds in the Carnie Trade* (Foreword by Teller) (forthcoming)

JEAN-FRANCOIS DUVAL, *Buk and the Beats* (forthcoming)

to the bar where I noticed a big blonde about 35, and alone--
well, about as alone as a big babe like that can get in amongst
8,000 men. She was trying her damndest to burst and pop out of
her clothes, and you stood there watching her, wondering which
part would pop out first. It was sheer madness, and everytime
she moved you could feel the electricity running up the steel
girders. And perched on top of all this madness was a face
that really had some type of royalty in it. I mean, there was
a kind of statliness, like she'd lived beyond it all. I mean,
there were some women who could simply make damned fools out of
men without making any type of statement, or movement, or demand--
they could simply stand there and the men would simply feel like
damned fools and that was all there was to it. This was one of
those women.

c.B.